SEO
MADE SIMPLE

Strategies for Dominating the World's Largest Search Engine

Emtrace Technologies, Inc.
3003 N 1ST ST
San Jose, CA 95134

by

Michael H. Fleischner

Emtrace Technologies, Inc.
3003 N 1ST
San Jose, CA

SEO Made Simple

2009

Published by

Lightning Press

Cover design by Greg Wuttke

Library of Congress Cataloging in Publication Data is on file with the publisher

Printed in the United States of America

To Jamie, Samantha and Alex-
My inspiration and joy

To my father, brother, and extended family

In memory of my mother

Contents

Section 3: Appendix

SEO Made Simple

Introduction

If you want to rank on top for Google, Yahoo!, and other major search engines, you'll need more than just plain luck—you'll need the exact road map used by those who have already achieved the top positions for their website(s). That's the purpose of *SEO Made Simple*—to provide you with a simple, easy-to-follow road map for achieving top search engine result placements for your very own website.

When I started out in Internet marketing no one was able to show me how to achieve the results I was looking for. New to Internet marketing the prospect of reaching the #1 position on Google, or any other search engine for that matter, seemed next to impossible. Of course there were marketing gurus and tons of Internet marketing products that offered "amazing results," and I tried lots of them. In the end many of these online products didn't live up to expectations. While trying to implement the advice given, I spent thousands of dollars creating and redesigning websites only to find that there was no single solution for getting top placements.

Although discouraged I never gave up. I knew that in order to be successful online I'd have to increase the natural search engine placements for my website. Through a good deal of hard work and persistence, I discovered the search engine optimization secrets I'm going share with you in this book. Now that I've achieved total search engine optimization success through years of trial and error and learning what truly works, I've decided to provide this information to as many individuals as possible seeking online success. Despite popular belief you won't need an advanced degree in search engine optimization or years of experience in website development to improve your search engine rankings. All you'll need is a desire to have your website ranked #1 on Google and a willingness to follow these simple yet highly effective techniques.

How This Book Is Organized

In thinking about all of this information and how to present it, I've decided to organize this book into two main sections: *On-Page Optimization* and *Off-Page Optimization*. Each section is designed to help you understand and implement the same techniques I've used to achieve top search engine placements.

Section 1: On-Page Optimization

The first section is your introduction to fundamental search engine optimization (SEO) techniques. On-page optimization covers everything you should do when developing your website and web pages. Don't worry if you've already spent money on designing your website or have limited knowledge of HTML or even website development itself. Once you know these techniques and understand how to use them, they can be applied in just a matter of minutes to any new or existing website.

Surprisingly many of these techniques are overlooked by 98% of all Internet marketers and those who are attempting to improve their search engine result placements (SERPs). How do I know? I know because when I review websites for a living many of them aren't applying these basic SEO techniques.

At the end of this section I'll provide a summary of the most important points covered in regard to on-page optimization. You can use the summary page for quick review or as an ongoing reference.

Section 2: Off-Page Optimization

The second section focuses on external factors that impact your Google ranking. These techniques are the most powerful, most effective techniques for improving your search engine results. In this section we'll discuss off-page optimization and I'll reveal the very techniques I use on a daily basis to increase website popularity, a key factor in Google optimization. After applying these techniques in combination with section one, your website ranking will literally begin to skyrocket toward the top of Google and other major search engines.

It's important to note that I cover off-page optimization in the second section of this book because without on-page optimization factors being implemented correctly, your website can never achieve top placement (okay, *never* is an exaggeration, but it would take much longer and require greater effort).

Again, at the end of this section I'll provide a summary of its most important points for quick reference.

Section 3: Appendix

The final section of this book contains some general information to keep in mind when embarking upon your SEO efforts and some helpful resources including an SEO glossary and checklist.

SEO Made Simple provides exactly what you need to begin your climb to the #1 search position on Google like I have for my websites. As each page unfolds, and you learn the most powerful techniques for search engine optimization, you will achieve success!

The Beginning

When I started learning about SEO I really didn't know where to begin. And like most stories of challenge, I was at my ropes end—I had tried everything. After many sleepless nights, nearly $20,000 wasted on website development, and a lack of results, I was tired, frustrated, and broke.

After spending many hours learning how to apply the techniques that the #1 ranked websites were using, I started applying many of the same techniques on my own website and quickly reached the top of Google for specific keyword phrases. These findings resulted in what I am now calling the *SEO Made Simple* method. My focus was—and still is—Google because it garners more search traffic than any other search engine. I've also learned that the optimization techniques used to reach #1 on the world's largest search engine are unique.

Shortly after I began applying these techniques to my own website, I quickly went from being on page 10 in Google for key search terms to the top of the search engine results placements (SERPs). Although search engine results vary from time to time, all of my keyword searches show my website on the first page of Google, and many of them are in the #1 or #2 position.

Did you know?

According to recent studies, the top three natural search results on Google garner more than 60% of all search engine clicks!

After spending many late nights applying the SEO techniques I learned, I found faster, more efficient ways of getting results. These optimization techniques saved me valuable time and money, making the process much easier and faster to implement. I'll be sharing all of these techniques with you in the pages that follow so you can avoid wasting endless hours on manual processes that can easily be automated.

As a quick aside, let me show you the results I've been able to achieve with the SEO Made Simple techniques I'll be teaching you. Search engine optimization is all about optimizing your site for a given keyword. We'll be talking about keywords later in this book, so for the time being all you need to know is that when you visit Google and search for something, the words you enter are comprised of either a single word or phrase. These words are called a *search term* or *keyword.*

Some of the keywords that I've optimized one of my websites (MarketingScoop.com) for include: *free marketing articles, marketing blog directory,* and *marketing expert.* Even though these keywords are considered highly competitive, I've been able to achieve top placements using the techniques I'll be revealing in the first two sections of this book.

See these results below. They are unaltered screenshots from Google. Alternatively, you can simply visit Google and type in the keywords I've mentioned. Please note that Google SERPs can change on a regular basis.

Keyword: *free marketing articles*

Keyword: *marketing blog directory*

Keyword: *marketing expert*

The best part of SEO is that I don't spend a single penny on Google Adwords or any other type of online advertising. Why would I? I'm getting all the traffic I can handle from the #1 placement on the largest search engine in the world—Google! Other keywords I've focused on include *marketing articles*, *marketing service providers*, and w*ho's who in marketing*. Feel free to check out my ranking on all of these keywords as well.

Here are just some of my traffic statistics, a direct result of being ranked first on a variety of search engines. The best part about organic search results is that once you're in the top three placements on Google, the traffic just rolls in.

I've reached top placements on Google with a basic understanding of SEO and SEO-related tools that give me an unbelievable edge over the competition who are trying to optimize for the same keywords and in most cases paying for their results.

Before we cover on-page optimization let's begin with a brief overview of the Google search engine.

What You Need to Know About Google

Google's the biggest—make no mistake about it. Global Internet information provider comScore, Inc. provides information on Internet traffic. According to comScore Media Metrix, using their qSearch service, which measures search-specific traffic on the Internet, Google sees more search activity than Yahoo! (#2) and MSN (#3) combined.

Below are figures about searching from comScore that were released to the public in the first half of this year. The pie chart below shows the percentage of searches done by U.S. web surfers at home, work, and universities that were performed at a particular website or a network of websites.

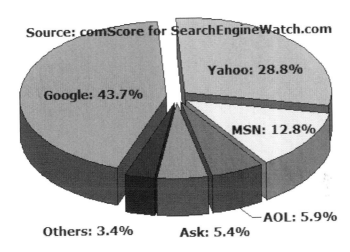

These figures are search-specific but not necessarily web search-specific. For example, a search performed at Yahoo! Sports would count toward Yahoo!'s overall total. Also note that some companies own more than one website. This means searches at different sites may be combined into one overall figure for the company's entire network. Here's some additional information:

- **Google:** Shows searches at any Google-owned website such as Google.com or Google Image Search.

- **Yahoo!:** Shows searches at any Yahoo!-owned website including AltaVista, AlltheWeb, and Overture. May show searches at some Google partners that show Google's domain in the URLs of their search results, such as Go.com.

- **MSN:** Shows searches at any MSN-operated website such as MSN Search.

- **AOL:** Shows searches at any Time Warner-owned website, including AOL Search and Netscape Search.

- **Ask:** Shows searches at Ask and any site within the Ask-owned Excite network, including Excite, iWon, MyWay, and MyWebSearch.

- **Other:** Shows searches that occur at other search sites.

Google PageRank Algorithm

What makes Google unique compared to other search engines is its unique website ranking algorithm, also known as Google PageRank or Google PR. Named after one of Google's founders, Larry Page, Google PR is symbolic of the SEO industry.

Google PageRank defines the weight, or level of importance, that Google places on a given web page. I've heard many people try to describe Google PR in various ways, but I think the most simple is in the form of a voting system of sorts. What's different about Google is that the search engine is based on a huge voting system where websites vote for one another. How do they do this? Each link that a site places on its website to another website serves as a "vote." Seems pretty simple, right? The more votes, the more important the website and the higher it appears in the search results! Well...sort of, but not exactly.

You see, in this election, not all votes are created equal—some votes hold more weight than others. For example, if a website with a Google PageRank of 7 (PR7) places a vote for a new website, that vote theoretically counts more than a vote from a website with a Google

PageRank of 6 (PR6) or lower. So votes from different voters are weighted differently.

Said another way, it's not just the vote you're looking for—you're also looking for the vote from the "right" person. In this instance, the "right" person is the website with the greatest influence (identified by a web page's Google PR). As a result, you're sometimes better off generating fewer links from sites that have a higher Google PR than many sites that have a low PR or PR of zero. You can determine your own website's Google PR by downloading the Google toolbar at http://toolbar.google.com and selecting the *Display Google PR* option.

Once you load the Google toolbar, you'll be able to view the PR of any site you visit. The Google PR indicator can be seen on the right-hand side of the following graphic.

In addition to the Google PR indicator, when moving your mouse over the graphic, text will appear that says something like, "PageRank is Google's view of importance of this page (8/10)." You would then refer to the webpage as having a "Google PR of 8".

Google Webmaster Tools Available

Google is one of the most innovative companies on the planet. They actually want you to succeed. Why? Because they exist to improve search. To support this mission, Google has developed a number of tools you can use to "improve" your online search experience and website.

I use the term "improve" lightly because the tools do a lot from a diagnostic perspective but don't do a whole lot when it comes to increasing your SERPs. Visit http://www.google.com/webmasters/ to view these tools. The Webmaster's area on Google is referred to as "Webmaster Central" and is displayed below.

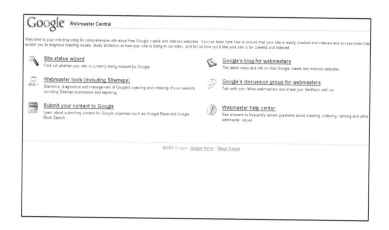

If your website is new, I would advise registering at Google and using the Site Status Wizard tool and even submitting your content to Google via Google's Webmaster Tools to begin collecting valuable information about your website. Once you've accessed Webmaster Content, you'll be able to:

- **Get Google's view of your website and diagnose potential problems.**
  See how Google crawls and indexes your site and learn about specific problems Google's having accessing it.

- **See how your site is performing**. Learn which queries drive traffic to your site, and see exactly how users arrive there.

- **Share information with Google to help them crawl your site better.** Tell Google about your pages: which ones are most important to you and how often they change. You can also let them know how you would like the URLs they index to appear.

Now that you know about the world's largest search engine and the tools they offer, it's time to start improving your website's Google ranking. These techniques can also help you improve your search engine rankings on Yahoo! and MSN. However, after applying the techniques revealed in *SEO Made Simple,* you will see the most dramatic improvements in your Google rankings!

Section 1

On-Page Optimization

On-Page Optimization

As I mentioned in the introduction there are essentially two parts to any SEO effort: on-page optimization and off-page optimization. We will begin with an overview and explanation of on-page optimization because it creates the foundation for your SEO efforts and is easy to understand. Simply put, what you do on your web pages can have a positive or negative impact on your search engine result placements (SERPs), — where your site is ranked on Google for a particular search term or phrase.

What Is On-Page Optimization?

Defined in its most simple form, on-page optimization is what you do on your website to help or hurt your SERPs.

The best part of on-page optimization is that it's fully in your control. And if done correctly it can improve how search engines see your website, weigh your relevant content (keywords), and place your website within search results for a given term.

Many Internet marketers debate the importance of on-page optimization when it comes to Google. I believe that the effects of on-page optimization are more easily seen with other search engines like MSN when taken literally. However, I also believe that any Google optimization effort cannot be effective unless on-page optimization is thoroughly addressed.

What I'm referring to when I speak about on-page optimization I'm referring to the proper use of: *meta tags, website URLs, formatting, internal linking, keyword development*, and *on-page placement.* Let's review each of these items in detail. I'll show you step-by-step what you need to know to ensure that your web pages are 100% optimized for Google and other major search engines.

Warning: Once you update your site you might very quickly find yourself ranked in the top five on some search engines like MSN. The MSN search engine loves on-page optimization!

Meta Tags

A meta tag is essentially a label that you give to your web page. Although there are quite a number of different types of meta tags we will discuss the most common ones. These "tags" or labels are essential for helping the search engines understand the name of your website's pages, know what information the pages contain, display a small description for search engine result listings, and understand how to treat each page when indexed.

Meta tags are important because different search engines weigh the information in these tags differently. It is believed that Google uses them in relation to other factors, ensuring consistency and validating page rank. It's good practice to make sure that your meta tags are complete, accurate, and up-to-date.

Note: Make sure that each page found on your website has its own unique set of meta tags!

Here's an example of the meta tags I use to describe just one of my many websites, **MarketingScoop.com**:

> <title>Internet Marketing Expert | Marketing Secrets</title>
> <meta name="**Description**" content="Internet marketing expert reveals powerful marketing secrets. Search our database of marketing experts, marketing service providers, and more.">
> <meta name="**Keywords**" content="internet marketing, marketing secrets, online marketing expert, internet marketing help.">
> <meta name="**Robots**" content="all">

You will notice from the example above that I've used four primary meta tags. These tags include the *Title* tag, *Description* tag, *Keywords* tag and *Robots* tag. More meta tags exist but these are the basic ones you'll need to use when thinking about improving your SERPs. Let's discuss each one separately and make sure you understand how to create each individual tag.

Title

This tag is the page title. Not only does it tell a search engine what the main theme of your page is, it also shows up as the title of your website on a search engine results page. For example, using the title above you'll see that it appears as the highlighted title in the Google results. The title tag also shows up at the very top of your web browser for each web page you visit.

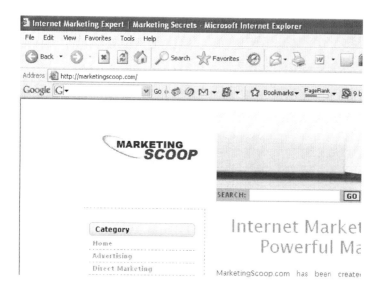

As a rule of thumb, make sure your title tag is *no more than seven words and less than 60 characters*, including spaces. This is the maximum number of letters and spaces displayed as a Google title. If your title is longer, it will run off and be concluded with three trailing dots when appearing in the Google search results listing.

The reason you want to limit your title tag to only seven words is because Google places a weight (level of importance) on each word in your title tag. Therefore, the more words you have the less weight applied to each word. This is why it's so important that your title tag contains the key theme of your web page or website and is focused on your specific keywords.

Note: Place your keywords in the title tag! I'll be covering keywords in the next section. For the time being, just remember that your title tag should include your keywords. Said another way, keywords are the search terms your potential customers use when searching for you online.

I've used two keyword phrases as part of my title tag separating them with a post (example: Internet Marketing Expert | Marketing Secrets). The post is found on your keyboard above the *enter* key. By separating these terms with a post Google sees them as being separate and distinct phrases without taking up valuable title tag real estate. Keep in mind that by using up to seven words in your tag you can develop many keyword combinations, mixing and matching terms. For example my title tag has helped achieve first page Google placements for *Internet marketing expert*, *marketing expert*, and *Internet marketing secrets*.

Description

This tag provides a description of your website or web page. When you enter a description for your web page it will show up under the website title in the Google search engine results listing.

I like to use my keywords in the description tag twice—yes, two times! This has a direct impact on my SERPs in MSN and related search engines. The impact to Google is minimal but does help with your overall optimization efforts. If you can, work your keywords into a description that seems natural and be sure to repeat your keyword phrase (see below). Your description should be compelling and accurately describe what users will find when they click through to your page.

Example of what to do:

> "*SEO Made Simple* can help you improve your **Google search results**. Read testimonials of those who have already improved their **Google search results** with these little-known Google secrets."

Example of what NOT to do:

> "**Google search results**, **Google search results**, improve **Google search results**, buy this book to improve **Google search results.**"

Overemphasizing your keyword phrase and stuffing your web page description can have a negative impact on your search engine results. Again, try to use your keyword phrase twice and no more. And be sure to generate a descriptive tag that compels browsers to click through to your website. This can provide a significant increase in the number of browsers who actually click through to your website from the search engine results page.

Keywords

The keywords tag is another way to educate the search engines about your website. There are a variety of thoughts out there today about the importance of keywords and keyword tags. My belief is that keywords themselves don't carry significant weight in isolation, but analyzed in conjunction with the overall theme of your page they signal Google as to the legitimacy of your content.

The keyword tag should include your main keywords, those you've chosen as the main focus of your website, as well as those associated with the theme of your webpage.

Note: *Avoid keyword stuffing.* When users place keywords on their web page or within their meta tags over and over again in an effort to improve SERPs, the search engines (like Google) actually discredit the value of the web page.

Here are a few methods of developing keywords for your meta tags.

- Brainstorm your own keywords.

- Visit the #1 ranked website for your theme or keyword and analyze their meta tag keywords. You can do this by simply visiting their homepage and selecting *View* from the navigation menu and then selecting *View Source.* You will notice their meta tags at the top of their web page.

- Use the Google keyword suggestion tool which is available at https://adwords.google.com/select/KeywordToolExternal. Type in the phrase that describes your website and be sure to note the top results which are the most popular search terms via the Overture network (more on this important tool later).

  This is my favorite method for choosing keywords. There's no sense in optimizing for a particular keyword if no one is using it when searching online.

  The other aspect of keyword selection you need to consider is competitiveness. Later in this book, I'll show you how to determine the competitiveness of a chosen keyword. If many sites are competing for the same keyword, it could be more difficult to rank well for and as a result, you may be better off optimizing for a different keyword phrase.

When listing keywords in their meta tags, some sites choose to separate each keyword with a space or comma. Either one is fine. However, I like to make sure that I'm not repeating the same keyword consecutively. For example, if I was listing marketing-related keywords like *marketing, marketing resources,* and *search engine optimization,* I would NOT list them in that order because *marketing* is followed by another instance of *marketing* when I use the second term *marketing resources.*

The right way to list these phrases would be as follows: <meta name= "**Keywords**" content="marketing, search engine optimization, marketing resources">. This creates a division between like keywords, resulting in a more neutral approach and avoiding potential issues related to keyword stuffing. If you fail to implement this properly some search engines won't fully index your page.

Robots

The simplest of all meta tags, the robots tag, signals the Googlebot (Google's search engine spider) to crawl your entire website. In order to index your website properly and include all of your web pages, search engines send their spiders to review and scan your website on a regular basis. Google does this every two or three days.

When the spiders view your meta tags and see that your robots tag indicates "all," they simply start crawling. Although some spiders would search the majority of your site without the tag, having it provides the added direction to search engine crawlers. Make sure the robots tag is included in your meta tags to improve crawling.

There are some Internet marketers or webmasters who recommend submitting each page of your site directly to the search engines via single page submission. This isn't necessary, especially if you are including the robots tag. Search engine crawlers do the work for you.

URLs

Many people believe that if you have a special URL, especially one that contains the keyword you're trying to rank highly for, you'll be #1 on Google. **This isn't necessarily true.** The reality is that having your keyword in your URL can help in some instances but is virtually meaningless in the overall Google ranking algorithm unless many other websites are linking to yours.

Let's explore this idea a little further. If this URL theory was correct, my site **MarketingScoop.com** would never be able to outrank the website www.marketingexpert.com for the keyword phrase *marketing expert*. At the time of this writing my site was in the first position on Google and the website www.marketingexpert.com wasn't even on the first three pages of search results.

So where does having your keyword phrase in the URL help? It helps with search engines like Yahoo! and MSN and when you're link building for Google. Each search engine has its own ranking algorithm, placing different weights on website criteria like URL, external links, and more. MSN is notorious for placing significant weight on the URL itself.

To see this in action simply go to MSN and do a search for *marketing expert*. You'll see that the first five results, and those that follow, all have *marketing expert* in the URL.

Another way that having your keywords in the URL helps is when it comes to link building for Google. Each time a website links to your website using only your URL, if that URL is comprised of your keywords, it provides a boost to Google search results. As I'll show you later, all linking coming into your website should contain your keyword phrase and this can be accomplished without owning a particular URL.

A great example of this concept is the keyword phrase "click here". Go to Google and enter the search term, "click here". If the URL theory was correct, that you have to have to own the URL that contains only your keywords, you would expect the first search result to be www.clickhere.com. However, the first result is for Adobe® Reader.

Why? It's because more sites link to Adobe Reader with the link text of "click here" than any other website.

Don't get hung up on this right now; we'll cover the topic of anchor text, link popularity, and link strategies in greater detail when we discuss off-page optimization.

Formatting

The manner in which you organize and format your web page can have a huge impact on your SERPs. I'm going to show you how to make sure that Google and other major search engines are reading the text of your page prior to reading "other" page elements such as navigational items. Additionally, I'll show you where on your web pages to place your keywords and in what format.

Did you know?

You can see what elements of your page are viewed as text by leading search engines simply by visiting your website and pressing *Ctrl-a* on your keyboard.

There are a few basic things to keep in mind when formatting your website for top Google placement. The most important elements include *content first, clean code (W3C, no flash), heading tags, alt tags, proper keyword placement, no flash* and *JavaScript external,* and *sitemaps.* If you get these elements correct, you can move on to address additional optimization factors.

Content First

When I originally designed my website for the first time, I came to learn that the layout was completely wrong. Even though I had my meta tags in place at the top of my coded page, search engine spiders had to sift through my navigational items (which were JavaScript, not HTML) before they could reach my keyword-rich content.

A great way to ensure that search engine spiders read your text first is to lay out your site with the appropriate content at the top. Search engines read from left to right and top to bottom. Many websites have a left-hand column that contains navigation links. As a result, Google will read all of the text in the left-hand column before the main content area of your site. The preferred method is to have Google read your text first so that keywords and other optimization factors are recognized.

In order to force Google to read the main content of your web page *before* the left-hand column, you need to structure your site appropriately.

Here's what you need to do:

Rather than creating a table to design your site that looks like this:

navigational links	Your body text...

You should create a table that looks like this:

	Your body text...
navigational links	

By laying out your page in the format noted above, Google will read your body content *before* your navigational items. Navigational items often are constructed with excess code and as a result prohibit search engines from reaching your optimized content. Here's an example of how to apply this technique using an actual webpage.

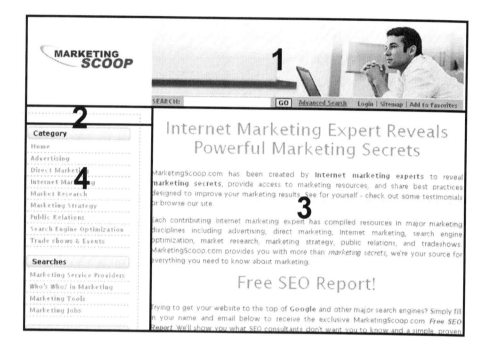

Proper formatting is essential for top placement in Google search engine results. If your site is set up incorrectly the search engines will read your navigational items first followed by your website content. As we discuss page elements and the importance of on-page items like <h1> tags and text formatting, you will better understand why we want the Google spiders to read your website content *before* all other page items.

Clean Code (W3C, no flash)

As mentioned previously, I'm not a programmer and in fact know little or nothing about web development. That said I know there's a right way and a wrong way to design a website. How do I know? I learned my lesson the hard way—through trial and error. Once I made the appropriate changes, my SERPs began to climb. That's how I learned the importance of proper formatting and coding.

If you work for a company or have ever made a call to a customer support representative, you know that businesses operate according to specific standards and service levels. The same is true when it comes to web programming. When dealing with website code these standards are referred to as W3C. The acronym W3C stands for the World Wide Web Consortium. You can learn more about the consortium by visiting their website at http://www.w3c.org.

For implementation of proper SEO techniques, you should verify that your website meets these industry standards. When visiting the W3C website you can learn more about W3C and even check to see if your site meets W3C standards by using their validation tool at http://validator.w3.org. I recommend using this free tool that provides specific feedback as to which area(s) of your code meet standards and which do not. Run each page of your website through the validator.

Any errors you encounter will need to be fixed by someone who knows the code in which your website was written. It is important for you to resolve the coding errors noted for a variety of reasons—not the least of which is that Google has an even easier time evaluating your website.

Note: Be sure to use cascading style sheets (CSS) when developing your pages. This helps keep your code very clean. Instead of placing formatting code on the page itself, make a call to your CSS, allowing you to reference all of the design-related elements you need across your website. Don't be too concerned if you're not familiar with cascading style sheets. Anyone who works in the area of web design has used them and can provide guidance when designing your site.

Heading Tags (<h1>, <h2>, and <h3>)

Heading tags (sometimes referred to as *headers*) are used to emphasize text on a web page. Search engines love to see these header tags because pages with large headings indicate the substance and importance of the content. Use the tag, either <h1>, <h2>, or <h3>, that's appropriate for your page and be sure to include your keywords in the tag. For example: <h1>free marketing articles</h1>.

Using the <h1> tag will display your text in a rather large format. The <h2> tag displays text slightly smaller than <h1>. The <h3> tag displays text smaller than <h2> and so on. Try to use at least <h1> tag on the page you are trying to optimize.

Don't overdue it on your heading tags. One to three is sufficient. The key is to make it flow well with your page and appear natural. Placing tags that make your text appear unnatural will only hurt your website's readability and click-through rate.

Alt Tags

Do you use graphics or images on your website? If you do, each image should contain an alt tag. An alt tag is simply the practice of naming a photo, image, or icon. You can check to see if your website images already have alt tags associated with them by running your mouse over the image. If an alt tag is in place, text should display. If text does not display, an alt tag is not present and needs to be added.

The literal benefit of an alt tag is that the text displays while your website images are loading, giving users information about the content included on your page. The primary purpose for alt text is to ensure people with disabilities can read the page. Blind users who use a page reader cannot see an image. The alt text tells them what the image is. The secondary benefit (or primary SEO benefit) is that Google takes these keyword phrases into account when evaluating your website.

The best way to tag your images is with your keyword phrase followed by the word *image*. For multiple images use slightly different wording.

For example, if you're selling widgets and optimizing for *discount widgets*, you would include an <alt> image tag for your widget using the alt text *discount widgets graphic*.

The code that would be used to insert an image tag in this example would be:

```
<img src="widgets1.jpg" width="125" height="60" border="0"
alt="Discount Widgets Graphic">
```

As with any optimization effort, don't overdo it with images or alt tags. Too many images can result in a slow loading website. Images that contain a number of alt tags, all with your keywords, can signal keyword stuffing.

Proper Keyword Placement

You must focus on where and how your keywords are placed on your web page. The frequency of placement is less important than once considered. Many people believe that if they fill their web pages with nothing but keywords, they can attain top placement. Search engines have responded to this and actually penalize sites that over use keywords. The number of times your keyword appears on a given web page is called *keyword density*.

The concept of keyword density gets thrown around quite a bit in SEO circles. It refers to the number of times your keywords are used on a given page as a percentage of the total number of words. Most website gurus suggest a keyword density of 2% to 3%.

Today, keyword density has less of an impact as it once did on your overall Google search engine results. Of greater importance is the placement and treatment of your keywords. Use the following guidelines to optimize your page:

- Place your keyword(s) in the Title tag, Description tag, Keyword tag, and Alt tags.

- Place your keyword(s) in an <h1>, <h2>, and/or <h3> tag.
- Place your keyword(s) in the first 25 words of your page.
- Place your keyword(s) in the last 25 words of your page.
- Bold your keyword(s) at least once on your page.
- Italicize or underline your keywords at least once on your page.

Note: A great way to get keywords in the last 25 words is by adding it to your page footer after the copyright. For example, "© 2008 Your Site Name. Your Site Keyword". Adding your keyword phrase in this fashion is relatively natural and appears virtually unnoticed.

Following these guidelines for proper keyword placement shows Google that your keywords are important to your web page and your website. It also helps you compete with other sites that are not as well optimized using these on-page factors.

No Flash and JavaScript External

In addition to ensuring that your website code is up to standards, avoid Flash and JavaScript on your page. In my entire career, I have *never* seen a site that leads with a Flash intro rank #1 on Google. If you can find one, I'd be surprised.

Flash intros do not provide keyword content in a manner that is easily searchable by Google. Even if the Flash intro was well developed and contained your keywords in some shape or form, the Google spider would not be able to read it. The whole idea of a flash demo, which is a self-contained entity consisting of dense code, is the exact opposite of what Google is all about. Google searches for open content that is easily read and navigated.

Is all Flash bad? Only if your site is completely Flash based or your homepage consists of nothing more than a flash presentation. If your intro page is largely Flash, I would strongly encourage you to replace it with an HTML homepage. If Flash is still important, provide a link to your flash script from your homepage. By doing so, you can optimize your homepage and then drive users to view your Flash demo.

JavaScript, a type of code often used for the creation of buttons, navigation, tracking, etc., is another double-edged sword. Using JavaScript can improve a user's experience but at the same time, it can have a detrimental affect on your SERPs.

My recommendation is that if you would like to use JavaScript, place the code in an external file. This removes the majority of JavaScript code from your page and brings your most important content (meta tags, etc.) closer to the top of your web page.

Sitemaps

A sitemap is a single page on your website that provides access to all other pages on your site, at least the most important ones. Sitemaps serve two purposes. First, they make it easy for visitors to find content on your site, and second, they enable search engines to spider your site much faster.

When the spider arrives at your website, it will read the first page of your site and then start looking at your navigational links (which include a link to your sitemap). When the search engine spider reaches your sitemap, it begins visiting and indexing each link contained on your map.

It's a good idea to have more than an index of links on your sitemap. Try to include short paragraphs of descriptive text for each link which of course should contain your keywords.

You can create your sitemap in HTML. Doing so is easy and only requires an HTML editor. Your sitemap should consist of a single webpage with links to your top level pages.

Some search engines require an XML based sitemap. Creating an XML based sitemap isn't difficult at all. In fact, Google has made it easy for you with more free tools. You can get started with Google sitemaps and other webmaster tools by visiting Google at: http://www.google.com/webmasters/.

There are a number of free programs on the web that can help you create an XML sitemap as well. Once you've created a XML sitemap, upload it to your server and submit it to Google Sitemaps through the Webmasters Tools feature.

Note: Don't forget to update your sitemap every few months or so. Your site changes, and so should your sitemap to reflect all of the changes you've made.

Uploading your sitemap to Google can have a significant impact on SERPs. Take the time to learn more about sitemaps and develop your own.

Internal Linking

One of the most important on-page optimization opportunities you have is to develop a simple and direct internal linking strategy. Internal linking refers to the linking structure your site uses to link to secondary pages on your website. Said another way, how you link from one page to another is very important. Many sites have significantly improved their rankings based on a strong internal linking strategy.

Internal linking provides direct access to your web pages in order of importance. The best practice for internal linking is to link to your main category pages from your website's homepage. To illustrate, I've created a fictitious website related to clothing.

In this example, our website's homepage is all about clothing and the types of clothing we offer for sale. From the home page you can access main category pages related to specific types of clothing. Once users navigate from the homepage to a given category they can read all about our products, prices, and how to order individual items. To facilitate easy navigation, our homepage has links to each of the category pages. This would look something like the following:

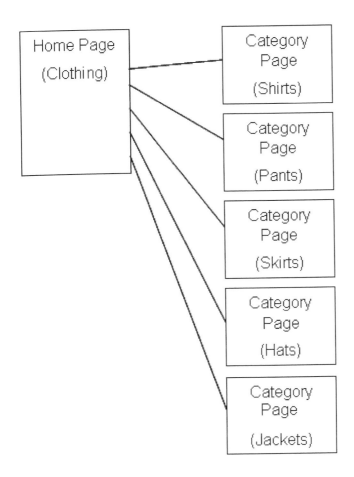

Although internal linking can be accomplished in a variety of ways, this is just one example of a basic linking structure you can follow. Here are some tips you can use to ensure your Internal linking is designed properly:

- Include links to all of your main category pages from your homepage by placing links in a navigational navigation menu. This menu should be available on each page of your website. Also, you can place links to your pages in your footer (see

Sample 1 below).

- Include your keywords in the links where possible. This tells Google what content can be found on the other side of the link and reinforces your internal linking strategy.

- Don't place more than three links to the same page on your homepage. This is unnecessary and could trigger potential issues with the Google search engine.

Note: Never under estimate the power of internal linking. Internal links are important because they allow for easy access to your content by search engine spiders and can transfer Google PR between pages.

Sample 1

Free Marketing Articles and more. To discover *marketing* secrets from an internet marketing expert or Search Engine Optimzation Specialist, visit the Internet Marketing category.

Home | About | Press | Testimonials | Contact Us | Advertising | Direct Marketing | Internet Marketing
Market Research | Marketing Strategy | Public Relations | Search Engine Optimization
Tradeshows & Events | Service Providers | Who's Who? in Marketing | Marketing Tools | Marketing Jobs
Message Board | Marketing Glossary | Free Marketing Articles | Article Submission | SAFELINK Program
Logo Store | Careers | Terms | Privacy | Marketing Blog | Blog Directory | Link Exchange | Sitemap

Keyword Development and Placement

Keyword development is the *most* important on-page optimization factor you will learn about and could easily make or break your website's ranking! But don't let that scare you. I will show you the best way to find the right keywords for your website and determine whether or not you can rank well for them.

Why are keywords so important? Because search engine algorithms are largely based on keywords—keywords on your web page, keywords in your code, keywords in the links within and pointing to your site. I guess you could say that Google and other search engines have keywords on the brain.

A keyword is any word or phrase that describes your website. Another way to think about it is in the form of a search term. What a user enters into the Google search box is considered a *keyword* or *keyword phrase*.

Let me begin by saying that choosing a keyword is more art than science. However, your selection of a keyword can be greatly simplified if you follow these steps:

1. **Define the content of your site in general terms.** What is my site about? Tennis shoes? Photography? Business services? Desserts? Once you've identified a general topic, its time to start your keyword research.

2. **Identify keywords/keyword phrases related to your topic.** To do so, visit the Google Keyword Tool which can be at https://adwords.google.com/select/KeywordToolExternal Note that the tool may take some time to load, but it will be well worth the wait. Google was one of the first websites related to paid search and is now the dominant player in search! This tool gives you an estimate of monthly keyword search volume across the Google network of websites.

The Google keyword tool looks like this:

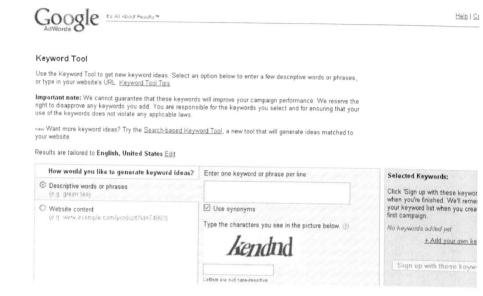

3. **Enter the keyword you're considering and press *Go*.** The
    resulting list contains all of the search terms and search
    counts—the number of searches using that keyword or
    keyword phrase performed during a given month throughout
    the Overture network. Results are sorted by search volume.

Your results will look like the following screenshot including a laundry
list of related search terms and corresponding search volumes:

Keywords	Advertiser Competition ⑦	Local Search Volume: March ⑦	Global Monthly Search Volume ⑦	Match Type: ⑦ Broad ⌄
Keywords related to term(s) entered - sorted by relevance ⑦				
tennis shoes		673,000	368,000	Add ⌄
tennis shoe		165,000	49,500	Add ⌄
mens tennis shoes		40,500	12,100	Add ⌄
womens tennis shoes		49,500	14,800	Add ⌄
women's tennis shoes		22,200	33,100	Add ⌄
men's tennis shoes		14,800	22,200	Add ⌄
white tennis shoes		22,200	5,400	Add ⌄
discount tennis shoes		4,400	2,400	Add ⌄
converse tennis shoes		9,900	6,600	Add ⌄

4. **Select two or three keyword phrases to research further.**
Okay, here is where the rubber meets the road. Look at your list and choose a few keyword phrases (not an individual word because, in most instances it will be way too competitive with many sites trying to rank high for that particular keyword) that represent your website. Make sure your phrases have a search volume of at least 1,000 monthly searches. Keep in mind that the more searches on a given keyword, the more competitive it may be.

Now you might be asking, "Why not pick the phrase with the greatest number of searches?" It stands to reason that the greater the number of searches, the greater number of visitors to your website. However, there are other factors to consider such as how competitive it will be to rank well for the given search term.

5. Determine the competitiveness of the keyword or keyword phrase (KEI). There is actually a formula you can use to determine the competitiveness of any keyword. This statistic is referred to as the KEI which stands for keyword effectiveness index. To determine KEI, simply take the number of searches performed on your keyword phrase and place it over the number of sites competing for the same keyword. You can find the number of competing sites/pages simply by searching for your keyword phrase in Google and looking at the total number of results noted in the upper right-hand corner of the search results page.

For example, if we were to choose the keyword phrase *women's tennis shoes* and do a search in Google, we see that 2,440,000 web pages (at time of publication) contain the phrase *women's tennis shoes*. To generate the KEI ratio, we divide the number of searches, 33,100 by the number of competing sites of 2,440,000 and get .013.

Most SEO experts would look at this and say that this keyword phrase is "impossible" to rank well for because the KEI ratio is so low—less than one. *I would argue to the contrary.*

The primary reason is that 2.4 million competing sites aren't that many in the grand scheme of the World Wide Web. I would say that any phrase that has over 1,000 searches per month with fewer than 3 million competing sites may be worth optimizing for.

Why do I say "may be worth optimizing for?" Because you need to do additional research to determine if the top-ranking sites are applying the *SEO Made Simple* techniques. This leads to our next step.

6. Research the competition. Regardless of which tool you use to generate or research your keyword phrases, you'll need to size up your competition. Remember that Google is a voting machine. The question you need to ask yourself is whether or not you can optimize your website (both on-page and off) better than your competition (and get more votes!).

Did you know?

There are a variety of tools you can use to research keywords. One of the most popular is called *WordTracker*, which offers a free trial version.

Example: Researching the Competition

Researching the top performing websites for final selection of your keyword is the most important step in keyword selection and it takes a little work. I will now show you how to research the competition using a real-world example so you can do it for your own website. Keep in mind, there is software available that can automate this process for you (I've included a link to it on http://www.myseomadesimple.com/secret.htm). Nonetheless, you should learn how to research your competition on your own to better understand this process of choosing keywords. Doing so is synonymous with learning to do division longhand before you start using a calculator!

Picking up on our earlier example, follow these steps to research the competitors for *women's tennis shoes.*

1. Visit Google and enter the first keyword phrase you are researching. Enter the keyword phrase "women's tennis shoes" and select *Google Search.*

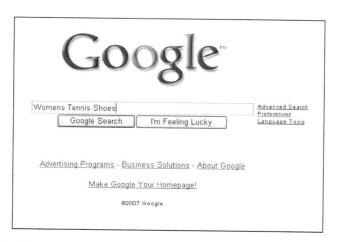

2. Identify the natural search results versus the paid search results. The natural results will appear below any paid results.

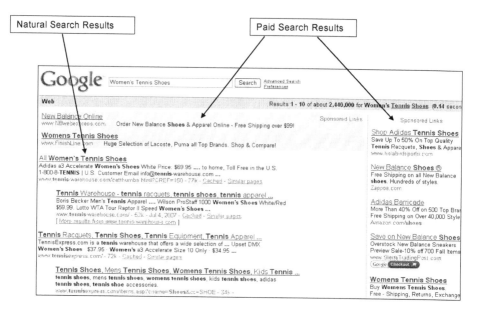

3. **Write down the URLs of the first set of natural search results.** The URLs will appear in green beneath each description. In this example, the first five natural results are:

- www.tennis-warehouse.com/catthumbs.html?CREF=150

- www.tennis-warehouse.com

- www.tennisexpress.com

- www.golfsmith.com/ts/browse.php?N=1548257

- www.zappos.com/n/es/d/35157.html

4. **Now you're ready to begin your site-by-site analysis.** You'll need to do the following for each site. I can show you how to do the first one—then simply repeat the same steps for sites two, three, four, and five. For each site, begin by recording the following:

- Website URL

- Google PR

- Number of sites linking in

- Keyword in <h1> tag

- Keyword in first 25 words of page

- Keyword in last 25 words of page

- Keyword bolded, italicized, and underlined

Let's do this for the first site:
www.tennis-warehouse.com/catthumbs.html?CREF=150

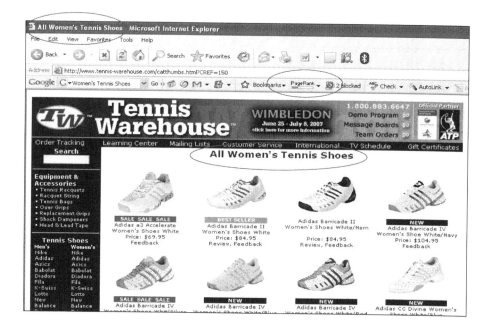

Begin by recording the Google Page Rank of this site. You can see from the rank meter in the Google Toolbar (you can download the Google toolbar at http://toolbar.google.com) that it has a Google PR of 4/10. You actually have to mouse over your PR checker in the Google toolbar to get the actual page rank.

The second thing we need to do is evaluate other on-page optimization factors we've discussed such as meta tags, use of <h1> tags, and so on. You can see from what I've circled that the title at the very top of the web page includes the phrase All *Women's Tennis Shoes* and the first header on the page says, All *Women's Tennis Shoe*s.

I also recommend looking at the source code and searching for <h1>, <h2>, and <h3> tags. To do so simply click on *Edit* in your browser menu, then select *View Source Code* and use the *Find* command. How many instances of header tags can you find?

Upon review, I noticed (see below) that the keywords are in the title but not in any <h1> or <h2> header tags. Additionally, I didn't find the meta tags that every site should have listing a title, description, and keywords—not to mention all the JavaScript that appears on the page. After some basic research, it appears as though the site we're researching isn't all that well optimized.

```
catthumbs[1] - Notepad
File  Edit  Format  View  Help
<html>
<head>
<TITLE>All women's Tennis Shoes</title>
<LINK REL=StyleSheet HREF=http://rs.tennis-warehouse.com/tw/std.css TYPE=text/css>
<SCRIPT LANGUAGE="JavaScript">
<!-- //
function validator()
{
var good, j;
        good = document.appfinder.xcat.value != "";
        if (good == false) {
                alert("Please select an Apparel Type from the menu.");
                return false;
        }
if (document.appfinder.scode_color.value != "") {
        good = document.appfinder.scode_size.value != "";
        if (good == false) {
                alert("To use the color option, you must also select your size.");
                return false;
        }
}
}
// -->
</SCRIPT>
</head>
```

I did find an instance of the keyword phrase in an <h3> tag but it was pretty far down on the page of code.

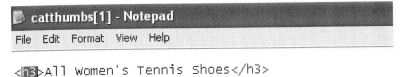

```
catthumbs[1] - Notepad
File  Edit  Format  View  Help

<h3>All women's Tennis Shoes</h3>

<p><table border=0 cellpadding=5 cellspacing=0>
```

Note: You don't need to be an expert in programming code. All you're looking for is whether or not the website you're researching is using meta tags and header tags (<h1>, <h2>, or <h3>) that include the specific keyword phrase you're researching.

So what have we learned about this site? It looks to me as though they are not fully on-page optimized for the keyword phrase *Women's Tennis Shoes* because they haven't followed all of the on-page optimization techniques we've covered in the first part of this book. This is a positive sign because if we chose to develop a competitive website, we could use meta tags and other on-page techniques such as <h1> tags, bolded text, internal linking, and proper keyword placement to enhance Google optimization. Lastly, the Google Page Rank of 4 is good, but over time, we could match it or even beat it with a PR5 rank.

See what I mean when I say that just because a site is considered "competitive" it may still be worth competing against using search engine optimizing? With the application of proper on-page and off-page SEO techniques, you could certainly out-rank this website for the keyword phrase *Women's Tennis Shoes*. All it would take is some time and proper application of the *SEO Made Simple* techniques.

Next Steps

Now that you've completed your analysis on the first website, you can continue your analysis by researching website sites 2 through 5 from our list of competitive sites. After doing so it's time to focus on off-page optimization. What you're about to learn is going to have the greatest influence on your Google search engine result placements.

Section One Summary

Here's what you should take away from this section about on-page optimization:

- ✓ On-page optimization is what you do on your website to influence SERPs on Google.

- ✓ Having the proper meta tags is essential. Be sure to include your keyword phrase(s) in your meta tags.

- ✓ The proper meta tags include your title tag, description tag, keywords tag, and robots tag.

- ✓ Choose your URL carefully. Your URL doesn't have to have your keyword included but it helps when other sites link to your site using only your URL.

- ✓ How you format your page is important for optimization purposes.

- ✓ Make sure you design your web pages so Google is forced to read your on-page content first.

- ✓ Verify that your code is W3C compliant.

- ✓ Don't forget to include your keyword phrase(s) in <h1>, <h2>, and <h3> header tags. This signifies the importance of your content to Google.

- ✓ Label each graphic with an alt tag that includes your keyword phrase.

- ✓ Place your keyword(s) in the first 25 words on your web page and the last 25 words on your web page.

- ✓ Italicize, bold, and underline your keyword phrase within your content.

- ✓ Eliminate Flash if it's the main presentation of your website. Google does not view this favorably.

- ✓ If you're going to use JavaScript to enhance the overall visitor experience of your website, place the code in an external file.

- ✓ Be sure to include a sitemap that's easily accessible by Google.

- ✓ Never underestimate the power of internal linking. A good internal linking structure can improve your SERP.

- ✓ Keyword development is one of the most important on-page optimization strategies.

- ✓ Research keywords and competing websites to select ideal keywords.

Section 2

Off-Page Optimization

Off-Page Optimization

As I mentioned in the introduction, there are essentially two parts to any SEO effort: *on-page optimization* and *off-page optimization*. Off-page optimization is even more powerful than on-page optimization when it comes to increasing your search engine results on Google.

What Is Off-Page Optimization?

In its simplest form, off-page optimization can be referred to as increasing a website's popularity. This popularity is defined by the number and types of websites that link to a given website or URL. I also like to think of off-page optimization as what you do on the Internet, *not* directly on your website, to improve search engine result placements.

The best part of off-page optimization is that there are a handful of proven techniques you can start using today to improve your SERPs on the world's largest search engine.

Off-page optimization is the most important SEO strategy for those seeking #1 placement on Google. Off-page optimization is the practice of increasing a site's popularity. The fastest and most effective way to achieve this goal is by developing quality links to your website. When I refer to "quality," I'm referring to links from sites that:

- Have an equivalent or higher Google PR than your site

- Include similar content to your web page

- Use related meta tags

- Have a large number of quality sites linking to them!

Even more important than the *what* (quality websites) is the *how*. Specifically, how these quality websites link to you is an essential key to Google dominance.

Your success on Google is DIRECTLY correlated to off-page optimization—the types of websites that link to you and how they are linking to you.

This is the biggest secret to Google dominance. Using this "secret" has changed my failure into success. Let me give you some visuals to reinforce the point.

Let's begin with a search for the term *free marketing articles*. You'll notice that the first search result is for the page of my website that includes my articles. This page is located at **MarketingScoop.com/articles.htm**. The keyword phrase *free marketing articles* is a competitive one with about 165 million other sites containing the phrase. You can see this by looking in the upper right-hand corner of the Google search results page.

The second and third listings on the page are for Psychotactics.com and Articlecity.com. Why is my site ranked first? The answer is simply that I have more and/or better quality sites linking to my website in the right way. It's really that simple because I've already taken care of my on-page optimization factors.

Google   free marketing articles   [Search]   Advanced Search
                                                     Preferences

Web   Results **1 - 10** of about **165,000,000**

Free Marketing Articles | Marketing Articles
Free marketing articles provided by MarketingScoop. Our free marketing articles are
written by marketing experts.
www.marketingscoop.com/articles.htm - 44k - Cached - Similar pages

Marketing Strategy
Welcome to Free Marketing Tactics: A Psycho Tactical Way to Achieve Morel marketing
strategy big and small business ideas Free Marketing Articles ...
www.psychotactics.com/free.htm - 13k - Cached - Similar pages

ArticleCity.com - Free Articles for Reprint. Free Articles for ...
to ArticleCity.com - your one-stop source for free articles. ... Internet Marketing In South
Africa By: Derek Robson Part 1 This article is written from my ...

Let's take a quick look at the websites linking in. This will give us a better understanding as to why my website is ranked in the first position. Anyone can do this by typing the following into the Google search box– you've gotta love Google!

Link: www.yoursitehere.com

Be sure to replace "yoursitehere" with your website or the URL of the website you're researching and press enter. Below you'll see a listing of all the sites Google has identified as linking into my website page **MarketingScoop.com/articles.htm**. In the upper right-hand corner you'll notice the number of in-bound links.

 link: www.marketingscoop.com/articles.htm   [Search]   Advanced Search
                                                                          Preferences

Web   Results **1 - 10** of about **117**

Free Marketing Articles | Marketing Articles
And without a doubt, one way **links** far outway the value of a reciprocal **link**. ... Directory
Submission Gets You Tons Of Quality - 1 Way **Links** ...
www.marketingscoop.com/articles.htm - 44k - Cached - Similar pages

Create an RSS Feed for Your Website | Syndicate Your Content
<link>http://**www.marketingscoop.com/articles.htm**</link> <description>Marketing
articles covering a variety of marketing topics</description> ...
www.marketingscoop.com/RSS-syndicate-your-content.htm - 23k - Cached - Similar pages

SiteProNews: Create an RSS Feed for Your Website Step-by-Step
... need to create an RSS file that contains a Title, Description, and **Link** URL. .... articles
(http://**www.marketingscoop.com/articles.htm**) like this one, ...
www.sitepronews.com/archives/2007/jan/24prt.html - 11k - Cached - Similar pages

Create an RSS Feed for Your Website Step-by-Step
http://**www.marketingscoop.com/articles.htm** ... Be sure to replace the information above
with your own feed **link** and image **link**. ...

According to this result, Google tells me there are 117 sites linking in to this page on **MarketingScoop.com**. Gee, I wonder how this compares to the #2 ranked website for *free marketing articles*. Let's take a look:

Google	link: www.psychotactics.com/free.htm	Search	Advanced Search

Web   Results **1 - 10** of about **50**

Marketing Strategy
If you would like to read up on a specific topic (and not have to scroll like crazy), please click on the bar above, or any of the **links** below. ...
www.psychotactics.com/free.htm - 18k - Cached - Similar pages

Links to www.psychotactics.com
www.wholinks2me.com/**links/**www.psychotactics.com - Similar pages

AHT: March 2007
Free Marketing Information http://**www.psychotactics.com/free.htm** Interesting laser project ... The following **links** are to a few of my favorites. ...
artist-how-to.blogspot.com/2007_03_01_archive.html - 92k - Cached - Similar pages

  AHT: Artist-How-To.com Update March 19, 2007
  Interesting **Links** ------- Gordan Parks Center and Photography Competition ...
  http://**www.psychotactics.com/free.htm** Interesting laser project ...
  artist-how-to.blogspot.com/2007/03/artist-how-tocom-update-march-19-2007.html - 65k -
  Cached - Similar pages
  [More results from artist-how-to.blogspot.com]

Ahh, only 50 sites linking in. Of course you must be thinking, "If I get 51 sites to link to my website, couldn't I rank higher than Psychotactics.com for the keyword phrase *free marketing articles*?" Yes and no. You see, it's not only the quantity of sites linking in; it's also, and more importantly, the *quality*.

Now, let's take a look at our third example, Articlecity.com. Logic would dictate that the owner of this site would have fewer sites linking in than the first site, fewer than the second site, and so on. With that in mind, let's take a look.

www.myseomadesimple.com

Wow! More than 75,000 sites are linking into this website. Then why isn't it first? The answer is easier than you think. The sites linking into Articlecity.com are either not of very good quality and/or are not referring to marketing articles in their link text.

If all of these sites linking in use link text that says something like *click here* versus *free marketing articles*, their search engine value to Google is extremely low for the search term *free marketing articles*. This is why I stress the importance of how external links are designed when pointing to your website. They must contain your keywords.

Furthermore, it's possible that many of these sites have a Google PR of 0. To find out for sure, you'll need to use an online SEO tool or software. Again, it all comes down to *link quality*, which is a function of Google PR, content alignment, sites linking into the linking site, and link text.

Link Types

Before going any further, let me explain the various link types. There are really only three types you need to know about: *one-way links*, *reciprocal links*, and *three-way links*.

- **One-way-links.** These are links from a website that is not your own. Also referred to as third-party websites, these sites place a link from one or more of their web pages to your website.

  Google values one-way links above all else. One-way links are incredibly powerful (if they're quality links) because you are receiving a vote from an independent third party.

- **Reciprocal links.** When you exchange links with another website, commonly referred to as *swapping links*, you're providing a link to their site (from your own) in exchange for a link from their website to yours. Reciprocal links are valuable, but not as valuable as one-way links.

- **Three-way links.** Three-way linking is when you partner with another website (site B) and provide a link from your site (site A) to their site. In turn, they provide a link from another site they own (site C) to your site. It looks something like this:

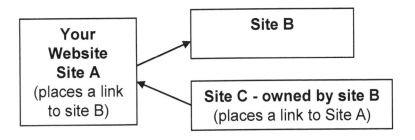

This form of link building is ideal because it results in a one-way link from a third-party website.

Which Sites Should You Be Getting Links From?

Now that you know the importance of links, the first question you must ask is where you should be getting links from. There are a variety of strategies to apply here.

The most effective way to identify the "right" sites to get links from should be based on who is linking to your competition which is defined by who outranks you on Google for your identified search term. This is a very important strategy and one that is frequently overlooked. You should be evaluating who links to the #1 search result in Google for the keywords or keyword phrases you're optimizing for and try to acquire links from the same websites.

Did you know?

If you get the same sites to link to your site in the right way, you will outrank your competition on Google for the same given keyword phrase.

There are a variety of methods to determine which sites are linking to the #1 result in Google for the keyword phrase you're targeting. Begin by identifying which site is in the first position for your search term. You can do this by visiting Google and typing in your search term. Record the URL of the #1 search result. Once you've identified this site, do one of the following:

- **Google search.** Go to http://www.Google.com and type in the following: *Link: www.nameoftoprankedcompetitor.com* and press return. Replace the "nameoftoprankedcompetitor.com" with the name of the site you've identified as having the #1 position on Google for your search term.

  The result will be a series of sites linking to your competitor. The only downside to this method is that you won't know which sites are more important than others (i.e., the number of links linking into those sites, Google PR, keyword content on pages, etc.) but it will certainly identify the sites you need to target for link-building purposes.

- **Alexa.** Go to http://www.Alexa.com and type in the name of the site you're researching. Alexa.com is a tool used to measure the popularity of sites based on the browsing activity of those who have downloaded the Alexa toolbar. Because not everyone uses the Alexa toolbar, the information is only directionally correct but provides a reasonable starting point as well as additional websites you can target with your link building campaign.

  Once you get the resultant websites, you'll see a number of options listed for each one. To the right of your competitor's website thumbnail image, click *Sites Linking In*. This option returns a list of sites that Alexa has identified as linking into the site you're researching. Use this list to target sites for link building.

- **Online SEO tools.** I have found that using online marketing tools to automatically generate a list of sites linking into your competitor's website, as well as link details such as Google PR, link text, page title, etc., is the most effective way to generate a list of targeted sites for your link-development efforts.

  I've personally bought and used about a dozen different products to help me keep an eye on my competition and, more importantly build an effective linking campaign. I personally use SEO software because in less than 30 seconds I know exactly which sites are linking to the #1 positioned website for my target phrase and receive information that helps me prioritize my efforts. You can learn more about the software packages I use at http://myseomadesimple.com, but keep in mind that using online SEO tools aren't necessary. You can often accomplish the same outcome without purchasing SEO software. The ultimate benefit to you is that many of these tools save you a significant amount of effort, reducing the time required for acquiring link building information.

You can use whatever SEO or link analysis software you want as long as it provides you a list of sites linking into your competitors and a way to prioritize that list. If you start to develop links from the highest quality sites first, your climb to the #1 spot on Google will happen that much faster.

- **Identify authority websites**. Authority websites are those sites linking to three or more of your competitors. If you don't have a SEO tool at your disposal, you can accomplish this manually using the following method:

  1. Search for competitive sites by visiting Google and searching for your most important search term.

  2. Create a spreadsheet of the top 100 sites "linking in" to each of your top five competitors (Microsoft Excel is a good tool for this).

  3. Sort alphabetically.

  4. While looking at the list see if any of the website URLs are duplicated across your list or use the "find" function. If the site appears two or more times, highlight it.

  5. Once you've developed your list of authoritative sites, visit each one to determine how your competitors are listed and how you can acquire a link to your website.

Model the strategy your competitors have used. If these sites are directories, look for a directory submission form. If the links are from articles that your competitors submitted, submit your own. If all you can locate is an e-mail, ask the webmaster to include your site. You may also suggest a link exchange if the opportunity arises.

If the website is already linking to your competition, they are a prime target for a link exchange or adding your link because they see value in linking to sites covering similar subject matter.

How to Link

Now that you know how to find the sites you want to receive links from, you need to learn the proper way to develop a Google-friendly link. Google-friendly links are links that increase the search engine results of a given website. Once we cover proper link formatting, I'll show you exactly how to get links from other websites.

I always cover the formatting aspect of linking in detail because your links are worthless if they're not displayed correctly on other websites. Let's begin with the anatomy of a link, for example http://www.marketingscoop.com

As a web browser, you would likely look at this link, know it was a link, and click on it if relevant to your search. This common application of link design is pervasive throughout the Web and used consistently (blue and underlined).

Another way to present the same link is with alternate link text. For example:

Marketing Expert

Link text can also be referred to as *anchor text* and is essential for Google optimization. Embedded behind the link text is an active URL. In the example above, if you were on a web page and positioned your mouse over the *Marketing Expert* link as noted above, you'd see the URL of http://www.marketingscoop.com embedded within. It is recommended to use link text instead of your URL whenever possible.

The question I often get is, "If you're trying to get links to your website from other sites, why wouldn't you want them to simply place the URL of your website on their website?" There are a number of answers to this question.

1. Your search result placement on Google is DIRECTLY correlated to the quality of the links pointing to your site *and* their link text.

2. A link that says http://www.yourcompanyname.com doesn't tell users anything about your website or why they should visit your

website unless you're a well-known brand. How can you expect to drive traffic if no one knows about or has ever heard of your website? Even if your URL is somewhat descriptive, you're better off with informative link text that includes your keywords.

Note: If all you did was develop a link-building campaign and asked third-party websites to place your URL on their sites (example: www.marketingscoop.com), you would improve your Google ranking for your website name (example: marketingscoop) and nothing else. Remember, you're not trying to rank well for your own URL, you're trying to rank well for a given keyword phrase.

To rank on top for a particular keyword or keyword phrase, you want third-party websites to place your link with the proper anchor text on their website. Your anchor text should include your keyword phrase (example: Marketing Expert).

The ultimate result is that when users search Google for the keyword phrase '*Marketing Expert*' as noted in the example above, it's my website that will show in the search engine results list because Google finds many links pointing to my website that say "*marketing expert.*"

One thing to keep in mind is that you should vary your link text from time to time so Google doesn't think you're up to any funny business. Adding some variety is good for all involved—browsers, webmasters, and website users. One way to do this is to use multiple keyword phrases in your link text.

Using an example from the section on keyword research and title tags, you can vary your link text by using more than one keyword phrase. For example, in addition to including *Women's Tennis Shoes*, we can add another keyword phrase like *Nike Tennis Shoes* and separate with a post (example: Womens Tennis Shoes | Nike Tennis Shoes). The post is usually found on your keyboard over the *enter* key. The result is that each time you get your link placed on a third-party website, you're actually optimizing for two keyword phrases instead of one! The HTML code you can use to get this effect, if you're not using a WISYWIG editor, is as follows:

```
<a href="http://www.yoursitename.com" title="womens tennis shoes"
target="_blank">Womens Tennis Shoes | Nike Tennis Shoes</a>
```

As always, be sure to replace http://www.yoursitename.com with your own website URL and obviously use the appropriate title including your keyword phrase. When engaging in reciprocal link exchanges, three-way link exchanges, or if simply requesting a link from a site, provide them with the link formatting noted above.

Make sure that every time a website links to you they are using the specific linking format (using anchor text that includes your keyword[s] or keyword phrase[s]). I can't tell you how many times possible link partners have asked me for a link exchange and submit their link to me in the traditional link format, example http://www.sitename.com.

Even though these potential link partners are on the right track in terms of developing in-bound links to their website, they'll never achieve Google dominance because they aren't asking me to place their link using their desired keywords as the link text. Applying the proper link formatting to your inbound links is vital to the success of your search engine optimization efforts.

How to Get Links to Your Website

As I mentioned earlier, building links to your website is the most important aspect of improving your Google search results—bar none! It also provides a significant boost to improving your search engine result placements on Yahoo! and MSN.

When I started out, I never realized just how important inbound links were to Google or how to acquire quality links to my website the right way. As a result I spent thousands of dollars, not to mention years of trial and error, to figure out that the more quality inbound links I developed, including my keywords in the anchor text, the higher I'd get listed on Google. When thinking about acquiring inbound links, those links pointing to your website from other websites, there are two key principles to keep in mind.

Principle #1: Quality attracts quality. When it comes to search engine optimization, if you take the time to do things right the first time, you will achieve your goal. An example of this would be the process of asking a related website for a link that includes your keyword phrase(s). If you send a form letter or brief email and ask for a link exchange you probably won't get it. However, if you take a few minutes to look at the website you're targeting and identify an opportunity to deliver something of sufficient quality (content, reciprocal link, etc.) you'll more often than not get what you're looking for.

Principle #2: Persistence pays off. As I teach you the techniques I've used to rank #1 on Google for even the most competitive phrases, think back to this principle again and again. Persistence is the key for achieving your desired result. A great example of this is some work I was doing for an online service company. After analyzing their website and suggesting changes, I quickly realized that my on-page optimization recommendations would never be implemented—largely due to a bureaucratic web development team and their inability to handle multiple projects simultaneously.

Despite an inability to implement my on-page suggestions, I moved forward coaching the marketing staff on the off-page optimization techniques for improving Google search engine result placements. They immediately started implementing these techniques on a regular basis.

Truthfully, nothing happened for about six weeks...and then WHAM! The techniques they used for building links to their website took hold and the results were undeniable. One of the keyword phrases that was most important to them went from the bottom of page 2 on Google to the #6 position—even without the benefit of on-page optimization.

Today, everyone is looking for a quick fix. When it comes to SEO, there are a number of quick fixes out there. These concepts are often referred to as *black hat* techniques and more often than not get your website banned from all the major search engines. Achieving top search engine placements is like losing weight. If you go on a starvation diet, sooner or later you're going to gain back all the weight you've lost and then some.

On the other hand, change you're eating and exercise habits slowly over time and you can create lasting health. The same principle applies here. Develop your links with a focus on quality, be persistent and you will achieve lasting results!

SEO Made Simple Off-Page Techniques

Let's jump right into it. All of these off-page optimization techniques will help improve your Google SERPs through link building, the most effective search engine optimization strategy available today. The more you use these link building techniques, the faster you'll see results. Don't hesitate—start using these off-page optimization techniques immediately to build quality links to your website and watch your Google search engine results start the climb to the #1 position.

Article Marketing

Article marketing is the practice of writing informational articles within a given subject area and distributing your articles to information-hungry websites across the Web. There are a number of article distribution sites you can use to distribute your articles to webmasters seeking content. This is done by registering with an article directory, adding your article to the relevant category on their site, and submitting it for review.

Once the article has been reviewed and approved, it is posted on their website for webmasters to copy and paste onto their own websites. **You leverage this *SEO Made Simple* method by including a link back to your website in the *About the Author* section using the proper link text (which includes your keyword phrase[s]).**

Each of these article distribution sites allows you to include an *About the Author* section at the conclusion of your article (see example below). You can see that I embedded multiple links back to my website at the end of this sample article. Sometimes the author section has a header that says *About the Author* and other times it just appears at the end of the article. Don't submit an article without it.

In this instance, I embedded two links, one for *marketing blog directory* and the other for *marketing blog*. Embedded in each of these links is a URL that points back to my website(s). For fun, see where my website MarketingScoop.com ranks for "marketing blog directory" as identified by the first instance of anchor text and where my blog (http://marketing-expert.blogspot.com) ranks for "marketing blog" as noted by the second link. You'll see top placements on Google for each of them!

The added value of article distribution is that in addition to getting links to your website from the article site itself, you also get the *viral effect* provided when others post your articles.

The *viral effect* is when a webmaster takes your submitted article from the article distribution site and uses it on his website including your author box. Over time, his web browsers may point to the article on his site or copy and paste the article onto their own websites or blogs if reprint rights are offered, generating even more one-way links to your very own website.

To see the true effect of article marketing, search on Google for one of my many marketing articles, "7 Proven Strategies for Improving Your Alexa Ranking." You'll find more than 500 references to this article, many of which are from quality websites. The result, because many of these sites have my Author Box included at the bottom of the article, is more than 500 one-way links pointing to my website with a single article! It's like link building on steroids. Each link builds my link popularity and is essential for improving Google search results. The best part is that this link-building activity costs me little or nothing to implement.

What if you don't have anything to write about?

If you are struggling to write your own articles, there are plenty of tools out there that can help you create a unique article. If you're not in the market for this type of software, you can also hire a ghostwriter or freelancer. I would recommend finding someone through elance.com or getafreelancer.com. You could likely negotiate with someone depending on your topic and pay as little as $15 per article.

Having original articles written for you can be worth *every* cent! Overall, article marketing has created thousands of links back to my website. In fact, if you Google my name *Michael Fleischner,* you'll find tens of thousands of references. Most of these references are directly associated to my article marketing. Begin writing articles today and submitting to article directories. You'll be glad you did. For the latest on article marketing and issues related with duplicate content, visit http://www.myseomadesimple.com/secret.htm.

Here's a list of the most popular article directories you can submit your articles to. There are hundreds more, but these are some of the most popular.

1. http://www.goarticles.com

2. http://www.ezinearticles.com

3. http://www.articlecity.com

4. http://www.amazines.com

5. http://www.articledashboard.com

6. http://www.article-directory.net

7. http://www.submityourarticle.com/articles

8. http://www.magportal.com

9. http://www.isnare.com

10. http://www.article-hangout.com

11. http://www.webarticles.com

12. http://www.articlecube.com

13. http://articles4content.com

14. http://www.article-buzz.com

15. http://www.free-articles-zone.com

16. http://www.newarticlesonline.com

17. http://www.articlealley.com

18. http://www.ideamarketers.com

Place Free Articles on Your Website with Reprint Rights

Another way to optimize your own content is to post your authored articles on your own website with reprint instructions (I suggest doing this before submitting to article directories). This allows your website browsers to repurpose your content under specific terms and conditions and search engines to recognize you as the original author – a very important step for improving search engine rankings.

Create a single page on your website that lists all of your articles. On this page, provide instructions on how your articles can be used. For example:

You're welcome to reprint these articles on your website and in your e-newsletters free of charge, provided that:

- *you don't change the article in any way and you include the byline (including a link to our website)*

In doing so you agree to indemnify [your website name here] and its directors, officers, employees, and agents from and against all losses, claims, damages, and liabilities that arise out of their use.

Note: By viewing and copying the source of this article, you'll be able to retain all formatting.

In addition, or in lieu of the message above, you may want to repeat a similar disclaimer at the footer of each posted article. For example:

Publishing Rights: You may republish this article in your website, newsletter, or book, on the condition that you agree to leave the article, author's signature, and all links completely intact.

Article marketing is one of the fastest and most powerful ways to build links to your website. Again, remember that you want quality links, so take your article writing seriously. I suggest creating 1 -2 articles per week and distributing them to at least 25 – 30 article directories. This can increase your SERP's both short and long-term.

Link Exchanges/Link Requests

One of the fastest ways to build links to your website, and therefore link popularity, is through *reciprocal linking*. Reciprocal links are created when two websites agree to link to each other. Reciprocal links are also known as *link swaps, link exchanges*, and *link partners*. When I was first starting out in search engine optimization I used reciprocal linking to establish a number of quality links to my website.

The challenge here is that a reciprocal link is really only valuable if the Google PR of the site that's linking to you is greater or equal to the Google PR of your own website. That's not to say that links from sites with a low PR don't provide value. In fact, when you're starting out, every inbound link with a Google PR greater than zero helps!

When you're developing reciprocal links, seek out websites that are contextually relevant to yours. In other words, if your site is about clothing, seek out other sites dedicated to apparel. These sites will tend to have similar content (keywords) as your site embedded in title tags, body copy, on-page links, and so on. Google favors links from sites that share the same or similar theme as your website, increasing the value of each incoming link.

Reciprocal Links and How to Get Them

Before asking any site for a link exchange, you'll need to develop a links page on your own website. A links page, also referred to as a partner page, is where you'll be placing the links to those sites that place one or more of your links on their website. As a rule of thumb, never include more than 100 links on your links page, as Google may consider your page to be a link farm. Link farms are in the business of posting links to other sites for a fee. And most importantly, **be sure to place a link to your links page directly from your home page.**

Linking from your home page will transfer the Google PR of your home page, which usually has the highest Page Rank of any page on your website to your links page—making it all that more valuable to potential link partners.

After you've created a page to place links on, it's time to find some link exchange partners. Begin by identifying a site that would be an appropriate link partner (see **Which Sites Should You Be Getting Links From?**). E-mail the webmaster of the site by locating a *Contact Us* button or form or the webmaster's e-mail address.

Before you send an e-mail requesting a link exchange, place a link to the targeted website on your links page. Doing so shows the webmaster of the site you're contacting that you're serious about a link exchange and that you're willing to take the first step. If the webmaster says no, you can always remove their link from your links page. Here is a sample e-mail you can use when contacting webmasters:

Dear Webmaster,

My name is _____ and I am the webmaster of www.yoursitehere.com. I have visited your site www.theirwebsiteurlhere.com and believe it would be a valuable resource for my website browsers.

I'd like to exchange links with you and have already added a link to your website on my links page at www.yourlinkspage.com. I would ask that you provide a link back to my website. Doing so would offer a valuable resource to your website's visitors and increase website popularity for both of us.

If you are interested in exchanging links, please add the following details to your website and let me know when you have done so. The details of our site are given below:

Title: Your keyword phrase here | Second keyword phrase here

URL: www.yourwebsite.com

Description: [Place a description of your website here. Make sure you include your primary keyword phrase at least two times in a manner that seems natural].

Alternatively, you can just copy the html code

<a href=http://www.yourwebsite.com target="_blank">Your keyword phrase | Second keyword phrase</a> *Place a description of your website here. Make sure you include your primary keyword phrase at least two times in a manner that seems natural.*

If you are not interested in completing a link exchange at this time, please let us know and we will remove your link from our links page. Thank you for your consideration.

Kind Regards
[your first name]
webmaster@yourwebsite.com

Feel free to modify this e-mail as you like. The key is to sound genuine and act in good faith. As I mentioned in principle #1, quality attracts quality and #2, persistence pays off. You'll receive more no answeres than yes answers, but over time yes' add up and you'll have plenty of quality links to your website!

Based on the type of website, and how well established your site is, you may consider sending a link request without the promise of a reciprocal link. A one-way link is more valuable than a reciprocal link, but websites aren't always willing to provide you with one unless they see you as a well-established authority website.

On a final note, once you establish a link exchange, check back regularly to make sure the reciprocal link is in place. If your link has been removed, contact the webmaster to inquire as to why your link was removed. Keep in mind that you want the value of the inbound links to your links page to be greater than the value of the outbound links; always make sure a reciprocal link is in place or remove the site from your links page.

Directory Submission

If you're going to own and operate a website, you must take the time to submit your website to well-established website directories. There are tons of websites out there called website directories that list other websites and website details. Directory submission is a great way to generate hundreds of one-way links to your website.

Some directories may charge you to be listed in their directory of sites. This fee is often used to pay an editorial staff to review and post your listing, but it may also serve as the price of getting your link posted on a website that has an established Google PR. In essence you're buying page rank. The one thing to keep in mind is that Google has begun penalizing "paid links". As a result, you want to limit the number of links you acquire through paid directories.

There are two types of website directories on the Internet: *human-edited* and *automated*. Human-edited directories review each submission by hand. These directories are of high quality and command a top Google PR. The most popular of all human-edited directories is DMOZ.com. In fact, even Google uses DMOZ for the Google Directory at http://directory.google.com/.

Automated directories are basically a dime a dozen. I don't mean to diminish the value of these directories, but you certainly have to make sure you get what you pay for. Even if a directory submission is free, you want to make sure that you are submitting to *quality* directories, sites with an established Google PR, strong Alexa ranking, appropriate categories, etc.

Another aspect to consider is that many human and automated directories work on a concept of link exchange. To get listed in their directory, you must provide a link to the directory from your website. In this situation, you should first check to see the PR value of the page in which you will be listed. Only submit your website to the directory if the Google PR of the page (where your website will be listed) is equal to or greater than the PR of your links page.

Start your directory submissions with the largest free directories:

DMOZ
A huge directory that's used by many other websites and managed by a system of volunteer editors. Please note that it can take a long time to get your site considered.
www.dmoz.org/add.html

Google
No charge for any site to list. Google finds your site whether you manually submit or not but it's definitely worth letting them know you're there.

www.google.com/addurl

Yahoo!
Noncommercial sites may be submitted for free consideration. Commercial sites require an annual payment of $299.

http://search.yahoo.com/info/submit.html

Then move onto Fee-Based Directories (there are thousands but these are the ones I recommend):

Gimpsy (Free/Charge: $30 one-time fee)

Interesting directory with a slightly different layout. Free listings have a long waiting period.

www.gimpsy.com/gimpsy/searcher/suggest.php

JoeAnt (Charge: $39.99 one-time fee)

Directory run by volunteer editors.

www.joeant.com/suggest.html

GoGuides (Charge: $39.99 one-time fee)

Directory run by volunteer editors.

www.goguides.org/info/addurl.htm

There are other well-known directories like Best of the Web and Aviva but they charge upwards of $79 to be listed. You're more than welcome to spend the money, but I suggest you exhaust all other link-building strategies first.

One of the best ways to find free directories to submit your link to is with directory submission software. I've used a variety of them to make the task of finding and submitting to hundreds of quality directories more efficient. Alternatively, you can seek out websites that list free Web directories. I've provided such a list on my website at http://www.marketingscoop.com/website-directories.htm.

Blogging

Build your own blog. Doing so is easy and provides a significant boost to your SEO efforts over time. Much like websites and website directories, blogs have their own directories and methods of optimization. Once your blog has a Google PR associated with it, you can provide targeted links to your website homepage and sub-level pages. You can start your very own blog in three easy steps.

After hearing about the popularity of blogs and learning about the multiple benefits of creating one, I set out to start my own blog a number of years ago. After doing some research, I found a number of popular websites that actually let you create and host your blog for free. What's even better is that the process of creating your blog is incredibly fast and easy. I suppose that's why blogging has become so popular.

Step 1: Choose a Purpose or Topic

One of the most important things you can do to ensure a quality blog is to determine the purpose of your blog and the topic you will be writing about. For example, a number of individuals who host blogs do so for the purpose of sharing their ideas on a particular topic. Others are simply looking for an outlet to make posts on just about anything without a real agenda. Often these individuals are simply looking to create an online journal or even generate revenue with Google AdSense (pay-per-click advertising).

Regardless of the purpose you choose, select a topic that provides you with the flexibility to contribute on a regular basis. You will often develop ideas for your next post based on the comments readers submit. This is one of the best ways to develop new content that is relevant to your readers and keeps them engaged.

Step 2: Select a Blog Provider

There are a number of websites that offer free blogs. The two largest and easiest to use are Blogger.com and WordPress.com. These sites have millions of users and have been offering free blogs for a long time. The benefit of using established blogging hosts is reliability and functionality. I personally use Blogger.com for my marketing blog where I offer a variety of search engine optimization tips and information at http://marketing-expert.blogspot.com.

Step 3: Launch Your Blog

If you're selecting Blogger.com to launch your blog, all you do is create an account, name your blog, and choose a template. From there, you can begin posting to your blog immediately. Many of the blog providers like Blogger.com give you the ability to choose from a number of blog templates. Advanced users can design their own blog templates.

WordPress.com, another blogging tool, is also very simple to use. After creating a username and entering your e-mail address, you create a blog name and title. You'll receive a confirmation e-mail that provides instructions on how to begin.

Once you've launched your blog and made a number of posts, you should really focus on generating traffic. Not only will the traffic support any online business you may have, but it can also improve the overall quality and Google PR of your blog. Some simple techniques for generating traffic to your blog include:

- Register your Blog with DMOZ, Google, and other blog directories (Technorati, etc.).

- Design your blog for SEO using on-page optimization techniques.

- Generate links to your blog via link exchange, article marketing, and traffic exchanges

- Update content on a daily basis.

- Use ping services like Ping-o-Matic to recognize new posts.

One thing you'll find about starting you own blog is that blogging is both simple and fun. As you develop a loyal readership, you'll find blogging to be a great learning experience as well. Simply put, there's no reason why you shouldn't start blogging today. Once your blog is up and running, place a link from your website's homepage to your blog. This transfers the Google PR of your home page to your blog. The next step is to link from your blog to your homepage using the proper link text, which includes the keywords you are optimizing for. This will obviously help your Google ranking via the inbound link-building strategies we've been discussing, but you should wait until your blog has an established Google PR before linking out to other websites.

Social Bookmarks

Social bookmarking is a way for Internet users to store, classify, share, and search Internet bookmarks. In 2005 and 2006, social bookmarking sites such as Del.icio.us, Diigo, Furl, Ma.gnolia, Netvouz, and StumbleUpon became popular. Soon thereafter, sites like reddit, Digg, and Newsvine began applying social bookmarking to news items, and now the concept of bookmarking is pervasive throughout the Internet.

In simple terms, social bookmarking is a way of tagging content on the Web (news, articles, web pages, etc.) for easy referencing by yourself and others who may be tagging the same content. This is very similar to using a bookmark when reading your favorite novel. The purpose is to make it easy to get back to where you left off or identify content you deem important. Social bookmarking works in much the same way. The only real difference is the social component—others can see your bookmarks and you can see theirs.

You can use social bookmarks in a variety of way to build inbound links to your website and therefore improve your overall site popularity and Google SERPs. What I personally like about social bookmarking is it's easy to do and very similar to other optimization methods I use.

The practice of bookmarking works like this: A user registers for a social bookmarking site (example: Del.icio.us). Once he has an account, he browses the Internet. When the individual identifies a webpage or piece of content he wants to share with others, he bookmarks or tags it by clicking a bookmarking icon. Once bookmarked, the bookmarking site keeps a record of the individual's bookmark and checks to see if others have selected the same content.

When others bookmark the same content it increases in popularity and is ranked higher on the social bookmark site, allowing others to see the most popular Web content as voted on by browsers from across the Internet. Some of these bookmark sites also let you view the bookmarks of others. Del.icio.us is famous for this; just type in the name of any celebrity and see what they've bookmarked (e.g., Pamela Anderson). That's what makes "social" bookmarking so much fun!

Bookmarking your own site on major social bookmarking websites is a great way to develop one-way links to your site and improve your Google results. I have found a great free tool, named *Social Poster*, that makes posting to multiple bookmarking sites easy. It can be found at http://socialposter.com/generator.php. This tool allows you to tag your site across multiple bookmarking sites instead of having to visit each one independently. You will need to register for each social bookmark site before bookmarking your own website.

After visiting these social bookmarking sites and bookmarking your homepage on each of them, consider bookmarking channel level pages of your site. Creating deep links into your site can enhance your overall Google rankings. And of course, make sure to use the proper link text in your site title and description.

One final word on social bookmarking: Now that you know how to bookmark your site, the next logical step is to make it easy for others to bookmark your site. To do this, simply add a social bookmark applet (free) to your site by visiting http://AddThis.com. They offer a small piece of JavaScript you can add to your site in the form of a button.

When users click on the *Bookmark* button they can view a dropdown list of various social bookmarking sites and select their preferred bookmarking tool to select your web page. This makes the process of bookmarking simple and easy to do.

Over time, as more and more browsers bookmark your website, the number and quantity of bookmarks continue to increase. These bookmarks serve as in-bound links to your website or webpage, helping to boost Google SERPs.

Press Releases

One of the secrets I've used to get my link distributed on hundreds of websites, almost overnight, is through press release distribution. The way this technique works is by distributing a press release—an announcement of news related to your website—containing links back to your website. Now you might be saying, "Hey, I'm not in public relations and I know nothing about press releases." That's okay; you can use the press release template that I've developed by visiting http://myseomadesimple.com/secret.htm and distribute it to media outlets across the Web containing links back to your website.

The most valuable press releases are newsworthy. When you share actual news, the prospect of that information getting picked up by online news outlets and distributed to hundreds or even thousands of sites can quickly become a reality. In my opinion the best way to create news is through an online poll or survey.

Option 1: If you're starting from scratch I recommend adding a poll question to your blog. The only reason I suggest adding it to your blog versus your website is that blogs usually offer tools like online polling with a single click. If you haven't started a blog yet, take five minutes to create one (including an online poll) at Blogger.com.

Option 2: If you have your own list (opt-in e-mails), use a tool like SurveyMonkey to develop a short survey and distribute it to your list. It will be the best 20 bucks you ever spend. You can find more information on this survey solution at http://SurveyMonkey.com. As always, you can choose any survey solution as long as you have a predetermined list you can send it to.

I would suggest leaving your poll or survey open until you've gotten at least 100 responses. Preferably you should target around 250, but 100 should suffice for your first release. Once you've completed your first survey and written your press release, you can select an online press release distribution service. There are a variety of sources that can distribute your press release and usually charge between $50 and $275.

Keep in mind that a press release is any bit of information that your prospective market would find of interest or value. For example, I've distributed releases when I launched my website and each time I collected information from an online poll. You could also distribute a press release each time you add a new feature to your site that delivers value or is unique to the market you serve.

Keep in mind that the purpose of your press release is to build links to your website. This is what Google needs to recognize and rank your site. As a result, you want to select a distribution option where *your link is active and you can specify the link text.* As you learned earlier, you must include your keywords in the link text if you wish to succeed on Google. If the press release distribution option doesn't include an active link, meaning a link to your website, select a different option or service.

I have used PRWeb for distribution services with my own press releases. However, PRWeb can get a bit pricey. If you're just starting out and don't have the budget for a top-notch service, I recommend using PRbuzz, PRzoom, or Free-Press-Release.com. They offer less distribution, but you can choose a more affordable option that lets you embed a link and specify anchor text.

Once distributed, give your release a few days to get picked up by the media and media outlets. The beauty of the press release is that "good news travels fast." After receiving initial media pickup, your release continues to be distributed for days and weeks to come. The press release, if newsworthy, is a fantastic tool for developing Google-friendly links.

RSS Feeds

Syndicating your own website content is a great way to provide information to your readers with little or no effort. Using an RSS feed, your updated content is delivered to individuals who have subscribed to your feed automatically and can include links back to your website and reprint instructions (remember, it's all about the links!).

RSS is a simple XML-based system that allows users to subscribe to their favorite websites. Using RSS, webmasters can put their content into a standard format that can be viewed and organized through RSS software or automatically conveyed as new content on another website.

A program known as a feed reader or aggregator can check a list of feeds on behalf of a user and display any updated articles that it finds. It is common to find web feeds on major websites and many smaller ones. Some websites let people choose between RSS or Atom-formatted web feeds.

Feeds are typically linked with the word *Subscribe*, an orange rectangle 🔲, or with the letters RSS or XML. Many news aggregators publish subscription buttons for use on Web pages to simplify the process of adding news feeds.

Choosing the Content You Want to Syndicate

Okay, so you're interested in syndication but aren't exactly sure what you should be syndicating. There's really no hard and fast rule here. However, keep in mind that anything you plan to syndicate via RSS should be unique, of value to a given audience, and something that gets updated on a regular basis.

Some individuals syndicate their content by placing an RSS feed on their homepage. As the website is updated and a new feed is produced, content is sent directly to subscribers. Others choose to provide a feed of specific content pages on their site. The choice is yours.

So How Do you Create an RSS Feed?

All RSS feeds are written using a code type called XML. If you're not familiar with XML don't let that scare you. I'll provide the specific code you need and instructions on what to do with it.

To begin, you'll need to create an RSS file that contains a title, description, and link URL. This information will be used by the RSS reader when individuals subscribe to your RSS feed. I've created an RSS feed on my articles page allowing subscribers to receive new articles each time they are published. You can too—simply follow these steps.

1. Go to your *Start Menu* in the lower left-hand corner or your computer screen. Click on *All Programs* and navigate to *Accessories*. There you'll find an option called *Notepad*. Notepad is a simple text editor that you will use to develop your RSS script.

2. Write the RSS script, which contains information about your website or content page and information about the content you'll be syndicating. To do so, type the following into Notepad. Replace the bold content with your own website's information.

```
<?xml version="1.0" encoding="ISO-8859-1" ?> <rss version="0.91>
```

This RSS feed should be viewed using an RSS Reader or RSS Aggregator. Firefox users click the Subscribe to feed icon.

Feed URL: **http://www.marketingscoop.com/**

```
<channel>
<title>Marketing Articles</title>
<link>http://www.marketingscoop.com/articles.htm</link>
<description>Marketing articles covering a variety of marketing
topics</description>
<language>en-us</language>
<copyright>MarketingScoop.com</copyright>
```

```
<item>
<title>How to market your small business</title>
<link>http://www.marketingscoop.com/market-small-
business.htm</link>
<description>If you own a small business, you probably don't have
a lot to spend on marketing. These simple techniques will help
you generate more referrals than you can handle. </description>
</item>
</channel>
</rss>
```

That's it. As noted above, be sure to replace the title of your website page reference and description. When you're done save your file by selecting *File*, then *Save As* from the top bar in the Notepad window. **Note**: Name your file with a .xml extension but be sure to save the file as text (e.g., http://www.marketingscoop.com/rssfeed.xml).

Be sure not to use any ampersands or quotes in your code as this may cause an error. XML requires ampersands to be replaced in the code with "&amp" and quotes with "&quot." The best advice I can give is just don't include quotes or ampersands and you won't have any coding issues.

3. Save, upload, and validate your .xml code. After saving your RSS file via Notepad, upload your .xml file to your Web server. This file should be placed on the same directory as your homepage or the directory of the page you've selected to syndicate. Now that we've created and uploaded your RSS feed, we must validate it. By doing so, we know that the feed is active and will work when individuals subscribe. To validate your feed, visit http://validator.w3.org/feed and enter your feed URL. The URL of your feed is simply the URL of the .xml file you just uploaded to your server. So, if your file was saved to your website's main directory and was called *rssfeed*, simply enter your website's URL, followed by /rssfeed.xml. Once validated, your RSS feed is ready to be syndicated.

4. Place your RSS code on your website. The best way to do this is to copy the RSS button **RSS** and include a link to the RSS feed you just created. You can grab the RSS or XML image by simply visiting a website like http://www.MarketingScoop.com/articles.htm and right-mouse clicking the image. Save the image (give it a name like RSS.gif) and copy it onto your server.

The code should look like this:

```
<a href="http://www.yourwebsite.com/rssfeed.xml"> <img border="0" src="images/rss.gif" alt="rss feed for my website" width="36" height="14"></a>
```

Be sure to replace the information above with your own feed link and image link.

5. Subscribe to your own feed. After you've uploaded all of your pages to your live site or testing server, open Internet Explorer and click on your own RSS button. You should be taken to a dialogue box that asks if you'd like to subscribe to your feed. Subscribe and confirm that the feed has been added to your list of RSS feeds (it should appear in a dialogue box on the left hand side of the page).

Note: If you're using Firefox, you will only receive a text page when clicking on your RSS button. Those using the Firefox browser can click on a small icon that resides on their browser navigation bar to add your feed. Additionally, the text file contains their feed URL which can also be used.

6. Ping aggregators to let them know that you've created an RSS feed. In order to let the Web know that your feed is up and running, you must give them a ping. This is very easy to do—just go to http://pingomatic.com and choose the appropriate sites to inform. Select blog-related sites if you're a blog and non-blog-related sites for other content. Complete the information and ping.

Another site you should ping is Yahoo! Simply visit the Yahoo! RSS submit page at http://publisher.yahoo.com/rss_guide/submit.php and add your feed URL. This will let the big boys know that you're syndicating.

*A **final note:*** Whenever you want to syndicate new content, you'll need to update your .xml file with a link to the content and a revised description. Once you've done so, upload the file to your server, replacing the existing .xml file, and the code will do the rest.

Another syndication service you can use is Feedblitz. I've implemented Feedblitz so that users can receive updates to my blog, article pages, and websites by registering with only a name and email address. Once subscribed, registrants receive an update via email each time I've added information to my blog or website. Feedblitz also offers syndication services. This is a great option if you are new to RSS feeds and would like to have your feeds accessible from a single location.

Give People a Reason to Link to Your Website

One of the best ways to attract one-way links to your website is to promote free content such as news or articles, white papers, free tools, etc. Ultimately, it comes down to offering something of value. If you do, other websites will provide one-way links, which are incredibly valuable for your Google SERPs.

Personally, I like to create article collections that provide a wealth of information to website browsers seeking information. For example, I've developed a posting of marketing-related articles that I have written during my professional career, placing them in a special free articles area of my website. There are a number of other websites linking to this resource, and as a result, I'm ranking #1 for *free marketing articles* and in the top five for *marketing articles*. I make sure to add new articles on a regular basis to keep the content fresh. Doing so encourages other sites to create links to the content from their own websites.

Another suggestion is the production of a small promotional ebook. If you've ever downloaded a book electronically from the world wide web, you already have experience with ebooks. When users know they can get something, even a small promotional ebook for free, they tell others. This creates a "viral" effect that is great for attracting one-way links.

If you can create an ebook of your own, regardless of its length, develop it in Word and save it as a PDF. As a last step, post it on your website and make available after browsers provide their name and email address. If you need help with your ebook or would like to leverage the work others have done, search for PLR-related materials. PLR stands for private label rights, and you can often "buy" the rights to ebooks, how-to manuals, etc. for little or no money.

The next step is to offer these PLR ebooks on your website. Before long, others will be linking to you because you're providing something of value. Just make sure they are linking in the right way. On your web page, encourage people to link to your ebook and provide them with the proper link text (e.g., If you'd like to link to us, please use the following: <a href="http://www.yoursitename.com" title="your keyword

phrase">Your keyword phrase ebook</a>).

As I mentioned at the start of this section, off-page optimization is the most important factor for improving Google SERP's. Use the SEO Made Simple techniques to build quality links to your website and watch your search engine rankings soar!

All of these off-page optimization techniques, when applied consistently over time, can significantly improve your Google SERP's and results on other major search engines. After implementing the various off-page optimization methods we've covered, select those you are most comfortable with and apply regularly.

Section Two Summary

Here's what you should take away from this section about off-page optimization:

- ✓ Off-page optimization is your key to Google success.

- ✓ Your success on Google is based on which websites are linking to you and how they link to you.

- ✓ Link quality is essential for improving SERPs.

- ✓ When engaging in a reciprocal link, make sure that the website that is providing a link back to you has an equal or greater Google PR. This is important for maintaining a favorable Google PR balance.

- ✓ There are essentially three types of links: one-way, reciprocal, and three-way linking. One way links, especially if they are from a page with a high Google PR are the best.

- ✓ The most effective way to identify the right sites to get links from is to identify who is linking to your competition. You can do this by using search engine optimization software or by using major search engines.

- ✓ Sources for identifying inbound links to competitors include Google, Alexa, and SEO tools.

- ✓ Use the proper link text when link building.

- ✓ Always include your keywords and/or keyword phrases in your link text.

- ✓ When link building, remember that quality attracts quality.

- ✓ Be persistent, take massive action, and the links will come.

✓ Build your inbound links with the help of:
- o article marketing
- o link exchanges/link requests
- o directory submissions
- o blogging
- o social bookmarks
- o press releases
- o RSS feeds
- o content or tools

✓ Give people a reason to link to your website.

Conclusion

Increasing your ranking on Google and other search engines isn't complex, but it does take effort. If you want to increase your website ranking on search engine results pages, begin by implementing the on-page optimization and the off-page optimization techniques you've learned in this book.

One question I seem to get quite often is, "How long does it take?" This is a difficult question to answer because it's relative. If you're trying to optimize for a keyword phrase like *'eating blueberries on a Sunday afternoon'*, it will likely require some simple on-page optimization and a few articles with links back to your website.

On the other hand, if you are trying to optimize for a competitive term, and the top-ranked website has hundreds of incoming links, it can take a number of months to reach #1 on Google. Regardless of where you're starting from, the key is persistence. These are the same techniques I've used to achieve top positions on Google for every keyword and keyword phrase that is important to my website. Visualize your goal and act as if you've already achieved it. Take deliberate steps toward improving your search engine result placements and before long you will be exactly where you want to be: dominating the World's largest search engine.

To simplify your journey toward the #1 position on Google, don't hesitate to use online SEO tools and resources. For a complete listing of the tools I use, visit http://www.myseomadesimple.com/secret.htm. Although these tools aren't required for achieving top search engine placement, they can help you get there more quickly than manually implementing particular SEO techniques. And be sure follow the strategies defined in this book. They've proven effective for my many websites and those I advise on improving SERPs. Best of luck on your SEO journey. And remember… keep it simple!

Section 3

Appendix

Glossary

Below are some of the most common SEO-related words, phrases, and definitions. For more SEO-related definitions that can help you improve your SEO knowledge, visit the marketing glossary at http://www.marketingscoop.com/glossarylisting.aspx.

Affiliate marketing - An online marketing strategy that involves revenue sharing between online advertisers and online publishers. Compensation is typically awarded based on performance measures such as sales, clicks, registrations, or a combination of factors.

Alt tag - The alternative text that the browser displays when the surfer does not want to or cannot see the pictures present in a web page. Using alt tags containing keywords can improve the search engine ranking of the page for those keywords.

Alt text - Short for alternative text, it is used with an image and has a number of purposes. Primarily it is a placeholder for an image, so that if the image is slow to load or not shown, there will be an indicator of the content.

Anchor - Refers to a link on a webpage, often found at the top or bottom of the page that allows users to move to specific content on the web page.

Anchor tag - Code determining the destination of a link.

Anchor text - The text part of any link, and of vital importance to any SEO effort. Instead of a link being displayed as www.marketingscoop.com, using anchor text will allow the same link to be displayed as *MarketingScoop*. The search engines will then index the page based on this keyword.

Backlink - A link from one site that points to another. When getting back-links always ask the person linking to you to use anchor text.

Banner ad - A graphic Internet advertising tool. Users click on the graphic to be taken to another website or landing page. Banner ads are typically 468 pixels wide and 60 pixels tall, but the term can be used as a generic description of all online graphic ad formats.

Black hat - The use of unscrupulous methods to optimize a website. Discovery of these methods being used will often lead to a site being banned from major search engines.

Blog - A contraction of the term *weblog*, it is a form of Internet communication that combines a column, diary, and directory with links to additional resources.

Blogroll - A blogroll is a term used to describe a collection of links to other weblogs. Blogrolls are often found on the front-page sidebar of most weblogs. Various weblog authors have different criteria for including other weblogs on their blogrolls.

Browser - An individual searching the Internet for information. Also, a software package (Internet browser) used to view pages on the World Wide Web.

Caching - A computer process that stores web files to your computer for later access. These web pages are displayed without the need to re-download graphics and other elements of the previously visited page.

Cascading style sheets (CSS) - Used to manipulate and easily manage the design of a website.

Click - Each time a visitor clicks on a website or website link.

Click fraud - A form of theft perpetrated against advertisers who are paying per click for traffic, in which fraudsters may use automated means to click on your ads from spoofed IP addresses over random periods of time.

Click-through - Term used to measure the number of users who clicked on a specific Internet advertisement or link.

Click-through rate - The number of click-throughs per online advertising impression, expressed as a percentage or exposure (often unique visitors to a page or page views). A click on a link that leads to another website.

Click tracking - The use of scripts in order to track inbound and outbound links.

Cloaking - One of the most popular black hat methods, in which the visitor to the site is shown a page optimized to his search request, while the search engine spiders see a completely different set of pages designed to rank well.

Conversion rate - The percentage of targeted prospects that take a specified action within a given time frame.

Cookie - Computer code that is embedded in your Internet history file, allowing websites to recognize you as a returning visitor.

Cost-per-click - A specific type of cost-per-action program where advertisers pay each time a user clicks on an ad or a weblink.

Cost per thousand (CPM) - A simple and commonly used method of comparing the cost effectiveness of two or more alternative media vehicles. It is the cost of using the media vehicle to reach 1,000 people or households.

Crawler - A program that goes through websites and gathers information for the crawler's creator.

Dead link - A link that produces a 404 error, page not found.

Deep linking - Connecting to a web page other than a site's homepage.

Deep submitting - Submitting all of your website's URLs—in other words, every page of your site—to a search engine. Most search engines forbid this practice.

De-listing/de-indexing - If search engines detect that you are using unscrupulous methods to get your site ranked, or if they regard your site as "spammy," they will remove your site from their index and it will no longer appear when users search for it.

Directory - A database of websites. Yahoo! and Open Directory are major examples. They are similar to search engines, except that the database is organized in a meaningful way by human beings. Many search engines use a directory as well as their own robots.

Domain name - The name assigned to a particular website (e.g., MarketingScoop.com).

Doorway page - A web page with content that's meaningful or visible only to the search engines; also called a *bridge page* or a *gateway page*.

Dynamic page - A page that generates content "on-the-fly" as a user requests the page.

eCommerce - An Internet-based business model that incorporates various elements of the marketing mix to drive users to a website for the purpose of purchasing a product or service.

Gateway page - A method once used to enable a site to rank well for a variety of keywords. It was frowned upon by the search engines and is no longer useful, as the search engines now base much of their algorithms on linking strategies.

Google - One of the most important spidering search engines by far, Google plays a dominant role in the search engine market.

Googlebot - The crawlers that index pages into Google.

HTML – Stands for *hypertext markup language*. The coded format language used for creating hypertext documents on the World Wide Web and controlling how web pages appear.

HTML e-mail - An e-mail that is formatted using hypertext markup language, as opposed to plain text.

Header tag - An HTML tag that is commonly used for page headers.

Hidden text - Text that is invisible to the human eye because it is the same color as the background.

Hit - When a person visits a web page, that web page receives a number of *hits*—one hit for the page itself, and one for every graphic on the page. The number of hits is not regarded as an accurate measurement of a website's popularity.

Hit rate - Also considered the conversion rate, it is the percentage of the desired number of outcomes received by a salesperson relative to the total activity level.

Homepage - The main page of a website.

Impressions - The actual number of people who've seen a specific web page. Impressions are sometimes called *page views.*

Inbound link - A link from another website to your website.

Indexing - Behind-the-scenes creation of an ever-changing database based on the contents of web documents; search engines and filtering software use indexing to find and/or block documents containing certain words or phrases.

Internet - A worldwide network of computer networks. It is an interconnection of large and small networks around the globe. The Internet began in 1962 as a computer network for the U.S. military and over time has grown into a global communication tool.

IP address - A unique number that identifies a computer or system.

ISP - Short for *Internet service provider*, an ISP is a company that provides access to the Internet.

JavaScript - A scripting language developed by Netscape and used to create interactive websites.

Keyword - A word that is entered into the search form or search "window" of an Internet search engine to search the Web for pages or sites about or including the keyword and information related to it.

Keyword density - Keywords as a percentage of text words that can be indexed.

Keyword marketing - Placing a marketing message in front of users based on the keywords they're using to search.

Keyword stuffing - Placing excessive keywords into page copy and coding such as meta tags; this may hurt the usability of a page but is meant to boost the page's search engine ranking. Hiding keywords on a page by making them the same color as the page background and loading tags with repeated keyword phrases are examples.

Keyword weight - Refers to the number of keywords appearing in the page area divided by the total number of words appearing in that area. Weight also depends on whether the keyword is a single word or a multi-word phrase.

Lead generation - The process of collecting contact information and identifying potential sales leads.

Link checker - A tool used to check web pages for broken links.

Link farm - A series of websites linking to each other in order to increase rankings.

Link popularity - Often used as one of the criteria to determine rank on search engines, the measure of the quantity and quality of sites that link to your website.

Meta search engine - A search engine that displays results from multiple search engines.

Meta tags - HTML coding that the user does not see, used to describe various features of a web page.

Navigation - Elements of a website that facilitate movement from one page to another.

Online marketing - A term referring to the Internet and e-mail-based aspects of a marketing campaign, which can incorporate banner ads, e-mail marketing, SEO, eCommerce, and other tools.

Open Directory Project (DMOZ) - A large directory of websites run by volunteers. Their database is used by many websites across the Internet.

Opt-in - A program where membership is restricted to users who specifically request to take part

Opt-out - A program that assumes inclusion unless stated otherwise. The term also refers to the process of removing one's name from a program.

Optimization - Fine-tuning a website or web page with the ultimate goal being to ascertain a higher position in all or a specific search engine's results.

Organic listings - Listings that appear on a search engine solely because of merit, applicability, etc. In other words, listings that are not paid for; also called *natural listings*.

PageRank - Part of Google's search algorithm, it measures a page's popularity and is calculated in part by analyzing the number of links to a page from other sites and factoring in the importance of those pages. The highest rank is a score of 10 out of 10.

Page view - A request to load a single HTML page. Indicative of the number of times an ad was potentially seen, or *gross impressions*. Page views may overstate ad impressions if users choose to turn off graphics (often done to speed browsing).

Paid inclusion - Paying to be included in a search engine or a directory index. May not improve search rankings but guarantees inclusion of pages a spider might have missed and "respidering" of pages periodically.

Pay-per-click - An online advertising payment model in which payment is based solely on qualifying click-throughs.

Pay-per-sale - An online advertising payment model in which payment is based solely based on qualifying sales.

Pop-under - An online advertisement that displays in a new browser window behind the current browser window and is seen when an individual closes his current browser window.

Pop-up - An online advertisement that displays in a new browser window without an overt action by the website user.

Popularity - One of several criteria used by search engines to determine ranking in search results.

Public relations - That form of communication management that seeks to make use of publicity and other unpaid forms of promotion to influence feelings, opinions, or beliefs about the company, its products, or services.

Query - A search phrase submitted to search engines.

Ranking - The position of your website within the search engine indexes for a particular keyword.

RSS – Stands for *really simple syndication*. A lightweight XML format designed for sharing headlines and other Web content. Typically, an RSS newsreader or aggregator is used to subscribe syndicated RSS feeds.

Reciprocal links - An agreement where two website administrators agree to link to each other's websites.

Refresh tag - A tag that defines when and to where a page will refresh.

Robot - Any browser program that follows hypertext links and accesses web pages but is not directly under human control. Examples are the search engine spiders, the "harvesting" programs that extract data from web pages.

Robots.txt - If you wish to control which parts of your site a search engine spider indexes, you can use a robots.txt file to prevent the spider from indexing certain parts. Not all spiders will follow it, but it can be a useful tool if parts of your site are not ready for indexing.

SEO - Stands for *search engine optimization*. The process of developing a marketing and technical plan to ensure high rankings across multiple search engine results lists.

SERP - Stands for *search engine results placement*. Essentially, where your website is ranked on a given search engine for a chosen search term.

Search engine - A server or a collection of servers dedicated to indexing Internet web pages, storing the results, and returning lists of pages that match particular queries. The indexes are normally generated using spiders.

Search engine submission - The act of supplying a URL to a search engine in an attempt to make a search engine aware of a site or page.

Shopping cart - Software used to make a website's product catalog available for online ordering, allowing visitors to select, view, add/delete, and purchase merchandise.

Site search - A program providing search functionality across a single website.

Skyscraper - A type of online ad that varies from a traditional banner size (468 x 60) and is significantly taller than the 120 x 240 vertical banner.

Spam - Unwanted, unsolicited e-mail, typically of a commercial nature.

Spider - A program that visits and downloads specific information from a web page.

Splash page - A branding page before the homepage of a website.

Stickiness - The amount of time spent at a website, often a measure of visitor loyalty.

Submission - Putting forward a site to a search engine or directory.

Thumbnail - A rough sketch or snapshot, usually of a website, that provides a small view of what a web page looks like in the form of a .jpg, .gif, or .png file.

Title tag - HTML code used to define the text in the top line of a web browser; also used by many search engines as the title of search listings.

Traffic - The visitors and page views on a website.

URL – Stands for *uniform resource locator*, an address that specifies the location of a file on the Internet.

Unique visitors - A measurement of website traffic that reflects the number of real individuals who have visited a website at least once in a fixed time frame.

Viral marketing - A phenomenon that facilitates and encourages people to pass along a marketing message about a specific product, service, or company.

Web analytics - The process of using web metrics to extract useful business information.

Web browser - A software application that allows for the browsing of the World Wide Web.

Web design - The practice of selecting and coordinating available components to create the layout and structure of a web page.

Web directory - An organized, categorized listings of websites.

Weblog - See *blog*.

Web metrics - Statistics that measure different aspects of activity that transpire on a website.

Website - A site (location) on the World Wide Web. Each website contains a homepage, which is the first document users see when they enter the site. The site might also contain additional documents and files. Each site is owned and managed by an individual or company.

White hat - A reference to proper SEO methods that are approved by the search engines. Using these methods for increases your chances of your site being permanently indexed in the search engines.

Whois - A utility that returns ownership information about second-level domains.

World Wide Web - A portion of the Internet that consists of a network of interlinked web pages.

XML feed - Simplified version of HTML that allows data (including product databases) to be sent to search engines in the format they request.

New Website Checklist

(Download at http://www.myseomadesimple.com/secret.htm)

PPL Marketing

Place an "X" next to each completed item

	YourWebsiteURL.com Keyword Phrase Here	YourWebsiteURL2.com Keyword Phrase Here	YourWebsiteURL3.com Keyword Phrase Here
Keywords			

Directory Submissions
Yahoo! Directory
Business.com
Entireweb.com
DMOZ.org
ExactSeek.com
Wikipedia

URL Submissions
Addme.com/submission.htm

Article Marketing
GoArticles.com
EzineArticles.com
ArticleAlley.com
Other

Affiliate Programs/Partners
Add to CJ
Possible Affiliate Sites
Other

Pay-Per-Click
Keywords

Email Marketing
Monthly Calendar
Direct Services Feeds
Newsletters

WEEKLY
Verify Link Partners
Evaluate SERP for keywords

Made in the USA
Lexington, KY
08 March 2010